United States
Department
of Agriculture

Forest Service

**Rocky Mountain
Research Station**

General Technical
Report RMRS-GTR-153

June 2005

Standard Fire Behavior Fuel Models: A Comprehensive Set for Use with Rothermel's Surface Fire Spread Model

**Joe H. Scott
Robert E. Burgan**

I0412155

Abstract

Scott, Joe H.; Burgan, Robert E. 2005. **Standard fire behavior fuel models: a comprehensive set for use with Rothermel's surface fire spread model**. Gen. Tech. Rep. RMRS-GTR-153. Fort Collins, CO: U.S. Department of Agriculture, Forest Service, Rocky Mountain Research Station. 72 p.

This report describes a new set of standard fire behavior fuel models for use with Rothermel's surface fire spread model and the relationship of the new set to the original set of 13 fire behavior fuel models. To assist with transition to using the new fuel models, a fuel model selection guide, fuel model crosswalk, and set of fuel model photos are provided.

Keywords: fire behavior prediction, fire modeling, surface fuel, dynamic fuel model

The Authors

Joe H. Scott has been a Forester with Systems for Environmental Management, a nonprofit research group based in Missoula, MT, since 1996. He is the lead developer of NEXUS, a system for assessing crown fire potential; lead developer of FireWords, an annotated, electronic glossary of fire science terminology; and codeveloper of FuelCalc, a system for computing, summarizing, and formatting ground, surface, and crown fuel characteristics from standard inventory methods. Scott has participated in several investigations of surface and canopy fuel characteristics. He has a B.S. degree in forestry and resource management from the University of California at Berkeley and an M.S. degree in forestry from the University of Montana.

Robert E. Burgan retired as a Supervisory Research Forester, Applications Team, Fire Behavior Research, Intermountain Fire Sciences Laboratory, Missoula, MT. He was one of the developers of the 1978 National Fire Danger Rating System and made the 1988 revisions of the 1978 NFDRS. Burgan developed the fuels portion of the BEHAVE fire behavior prediction system. He was the lead Forest Service scientist, working with scientists at the USGS EROS Data Center, to develop the greenness maps now used to assess fire potential nationally. He was the lead scientist in developing a national 1-km resolution fuel model map from the Land Cover Characteristics Database provided by the EROS Data Center. He was the initial developer of the Fire Potential Index and has worked closely with EROS Data Center scientists and others to improve and implement it.

Acknowledgments _____

We are grateful for thoughtful comments on the draft fuel model set or HTML application provided by: Collin Bevins, Systems for Environmental Management; J.D. Carlson, Oklahoma State University; Don Carlton, Fire Program Solutions, LLC; Corky Conover, Sequoia National Park; Wayne Cook, Washington Office Fire Technology Transfer Program; Dave Engle, Oklahoma State University; Kato Howard, Alaska Fire Service; Randi Jandt, Alaska Fire Service; Paul Langowski, USFS Rocky Mountain Region; Duncan Lutes, Systems for Environmental Management; Melanie Miller, BLM (stationed at Missoula Fire Sciences Lab); Rob Seli, Missoula Fire Sciences Lab; Dale Wade, Southern Research Station (retired); Dave Whitmer, Alaska Fire Service; and Robert Ziel, Michigan Department of Natural Resources. For their reviews of the manuscript we also thank Patricia Andrews and Mark Finney, Missoula Fire Sciences Lab; James K. Agee, University of Washington; Sam Sandberg, FERA Pacific Fire Sciences Lab; and Jennifer L. Long, Systems for Environmental Management.

Photos to illustrate fuel models were provided by Roger Ottmar, Pacific Fire Sciences Laboratory, Pacific Northwest Research Station; Bob Burgan, Missoula Fire Sciences Lab (retired); Joe Scott, Systems for Environmental Management; and other published photo guides.

Funding for the development of a new set of standard fire behavior fuel models and the preparation of this document was provided by the LANDFIRE project, USDA Forest Service, Rocky Mountain Research Station. This project was conducted under contract with Systems for Environmental Management, Missoula, MT.

Standard Fire Behavior Fuel Models: A Comprehensive Set for Use with Rothermel's Surface Fire Spread Model

Joe H. Scott
Robert E. Burgan

Contents

Standard Fire Behavior Fuel Models: A Comprehensive Set for Use with Rothermel's Surface Fire Spread Model

Joe H. Scott
Robert E. Burgan

Introduction

Predicting the potential behavior and effects of wildland fire is an essential task in fire management. Mathematical surface fire behavior and fire effects models and prediction systems are driven in part by fuelbed inputs such as load, bulk density, fuel particle size, heat content, and moisture of extinction. To facilitate use in models and systems, fuelbed inputs have been formulated into fuel models. A fuel model is a set of fuelbed inputs needed by a particular fire behavior or fire effects model. Different kinds of fuel models are used in fire science; this document addresses only fire behavior fuel models for use in the Rothermel (1972) surface fire spread model.

Fire behavior fuel models are used as input to the Rothermel (1972) fire spread model, which is used in a variety of fire behavior modeling systems. The fire behavior fuel model input set includes:

- Fuel load by category (live and dead) and particle size class (0 to 0.25 inch, 0.25 to 1.0 inch, and 1.0 to 3.0 inches diameter)
- Surface-area-to-volume (SAV) ratio by component and size class
- Heat content by category
- Fuelbed depth
- Dead fuel moisture of extinction.

The National Fire Danger Rating System (NFDRS; Deeming and others 1977) uses Rothermel's (1972) spread model as its core. However, there are differences in the calculations that require the use of different fuel models than those for fire behavior prediction. Therefore, there is a separate set of fuel models for use within NFDRS. This paper does not address NFDRS fuel models; they are not affected by this work. The fuel models described here should not be used in the NFDRS.

Rothermel (1972) defined a fire behavior fuel model as a "complete set of [fuel] inputs for the mathematical fire spread model," and listed parameters for 11 fuel models. To assist in understanding the sensitivity of certain inputs, Rothermel held constant the fuel particle properties (total and effective mineral content, heat content, and particle density). Extinction moisture content was not listed for each fuel model separately, but instead held at 30 percent for all models. Thus, variation in predicted spread rate among models could be attributed to fuel load by size class, fuelbed depth, and fuel particle size. Parameters for 10-hr and 100-hr SAV were listed for each fuel model, but did not vary among models – 109 1/ft and 30 1/ft, respectively.

Albini (1976) refined those 11 fuel models and added two others, Dormant Brush (6) and Southern Rough (7). His tabulated set became what is now called the original 13 fire behavior fuel models. Whereas extinction moisture content was held constant for Rothermel's 11 fuel models, Albini's fuel models specified this value for each fuel

USDA Forest Service Gen. Tech. Rep. RMRS-GTR-153. 2005

1

model. Albini noted that "other variables needed to complete the [fuel] descriptions are held constant for the entire set."

Anderson (1982) described the 13 fuel models listed by Albini and provided aids to selecting a fuel model. Fuel model parameters did not change from Albini's set. Anderson listed as model parameters only fuel load by size class, fuelbed depth, and dead fuel extinction moisture.

The BEHAVE fire behavior prediction and fuel modeling system (Andrews 1986; Burgan and Rothermel 1984) included fuel particle heat content as a fuel model parameter that could vary from model to model, whereas previous work had left that parameter constant. FARSITE (Finney 1998) and BehavePlus (Andrews and others 2003) allow the user to specify separate live and dead heat content values. The ability to specify heat content is primarily for greater precision when building a custom fuel model; the original 13 fuel models still used a single value of 8000 BTU/lb for live and dead heat content for all fuel models.

Although a fuel model technically includes all fuel inputs to the Rothermel surface fire spread model, several fuel inputs have never been subject to control by a user when creating a custom fuel model: total and effective mineral contents, and fuel particle density. The 10-hr and 100-hr SAVs were listed as model parameters for the original 13 fuel models but are generally not subject to control of the user when making custom fuel models in fire modeling systems. For the above reasons, we did not consider using values for fuel particle properties or 10-hr and 100-hr SAVs other than the constant values originally published by Rothermel (1972). We list as parameters only those fuel model inputs that vary among models:

- Fuel load by size class and category
- Live woody, live herbaceous, and dead 1-hr SAV
- Fuelbed depth
- Dead fuel extinction moisture content
- Heat content of live and dead fuels

For all fuel models in this new set:

- 10-hr dead fuel SAV is 109 1/ft, and 100-hr SAV is 30 1/ft.
- Total mineral content is 5.55 percent; effective (silica-free) mineral content is 1.00 percent.
- Ovendry fuel particle density is 32 lb/ft^3.

Need

The original 13 fire behavior fuel models are "for the severe period of the fire season when wildfires pose greater control problems..." (Anderson 1982). Those fuel models have worked well for predicting spread rate and intensity of active fires at peak of fire season in part because the associated dry conditions lead to a more uniform fuel complex, an important assumption of the underlying fire spread model (Rothermel 1972). However, they have deficiencies for other purposes, including prescribed fire, wildland fire use, simulating the effects of fuel treatments on potential fire behavior, and simulating transition to crown fire using crown fire initiation models. Widespread use of the Rothermel (1972) fire spread model and desire for more options in selecting a fuel model indicate the need for a new set of models to:

- Improve the accuracy of fire behavior predictions outside of the severe period of the fire season, such as prescribed fire and fire use applications. For example, the original grass models 1 (short grass) and 3 (tall grass) are fully cured to represent the most severe part of the fire season. Applying those fuel models to situations in which the grass fuelbed is not fully cured (that is, outside the severe part of the fire season) leads to overprediction.

- Increase the number of fuel models applicable in high-humidity areas. With the Rothermel spread model, the only way to accommodate fuel complexes that burn well at high humidity is through the moisture of extinction parameter. Only a few of the original 13 fuel models are appropriate for fuelbeds that burn well at relatively high dead fuel moistures.
- Increase the number of fuel models for forest litter and litter with grass or shrub understory. Predicted surface fire behavior drives crown fire models (Alexander 1988; Van Wagner 1977), so increased precision in surface fire intensity prediction will lead to increased precision in crown fire behavior prediction and hazard assessment.
- Increase the ability to simulate changes in fire behavior as a result of fuel treatment by offering more fuel model choices, especially in timber-dominated fuelbeds. This fuel model set does not attempt to directly simulate the effects of the wide variety of available fuel treatment options.

Scope

The development of a new set of standard fire behavior fuel models does not address deficiencies in the Rothermel surface fire spread model itself. Like the original set of 13, the new fire behavior fuel model set is applicable to fire behavior modeling systems that use Rothermel's surface fire spread model. Any description of the presence or absence of overstory trees is due to their potential effect on surface fuels (for example, needle litter in a grass fuel model).

Also like the original fuel models, the new set is for simulating surface fire behavior at the flaming front only, not residual combustion that takes place after the flaming front has passed. Other methods of describing fuel and other types of fuel models are used for prediction of postfrontal combustion, fuel consumption, smoke production, and crown fire behavior. The fuel model parameters presented in this set should not be used as fuelbed characteristics for fuel consumption models.

Finally, the same fuelbed assumptions of homogeneity and continuity apply to these as well as the original 13 fuel models (Rothermel 1972). Methods of addressing heterogeneous or discontinuous fuels are available in fire modeling systems.

Development

We compiled fuel complex information from several volumes of the Natural Fuels Photo Series (Ottmar and Vihnanek 1998, 1999, 2000, 2002; Ottmar and others 1998, 2000, 2002, 2003; Wright and others 2002) and other sources. The range of fuel complex characteristics suggested the range of fuel conditions for which fuel models were needed. We subjectively assigned a fire-carrying fuel type and dead fuel extinction moisture content to each fuel complex, then grouped the complexes by fine fuel load, fuel type, and extinction moisture. We created one fuel model for each of the approximately 60 groups. Surface-area-to-volume ratio for 1-hr timelag, live herbaceous and live woody classes were assigned subjectively for each draft fuel model. Fuelbed depth was assigned after subjective interpretation of fuel complex data and visual inspection of photographs. Heat content of live and dead fuels is 8000 BTU/lb for all fuel models except GR6 (High Load, Humid Climate Grass), which is 9000 BTU/lb for both live and dead fuels.

Next, we made fire behavior simulations over a range of midflame wind speeds and several fuel moisture scenarios. Although the groups of fuel complexes appeared to be distinct from one another, the fuel models we created from them often led to similar flame length and rate of spread, so several models were eliminated. Also, after comparing fire

USDA Forest Service Gen. Tech. Rep. RMRS-GTR-153. 2005

3

behavior outputs from the draft fuel model set with outputs from the original 13 fuel models, we added stylized fuel models to simulate specific fire behavior characteristics not simulated by any of the draft models. Finally, we adjusted the parameters of many draft fuel models to better coordinate fire behavior outputs of related fuel models.

The draft fuel model set was sent to more than three dozen fire science researchers and managers for review; their comments were incorporated into the final fuel model set and its documentation, which was reviewed again by a smaller cadre.

Characteristics

This new set of standard fire behavior fuel models is designed to stand alone; none of the original 13 fire behavior fuel models is repeated in the new set; the fuel model selection guide points to the new fuel models only. However, the original 13 fire behavior fuel models will still be available, and they are still called fire behavior fuel models 1-13. There is no immediate need to reanalyze existing fuel model maps or lookup tables that are sufficient for their purpose. However, we anticipate that new fuel model mapping projects will use this new set rather than the original 13.

Documentation and naming of the new fuel models refer to fuel or fuel types, not vegetation or vegetation types. For example, what was formerly termed a "Chaparral" fuel model might now be called a "Heavy Load, Tall Brush" model because one fuel model can be applied in many vegetation types. Likewise, the fuel model selection guide does not refer to specific vegetation types except as necessary to illustrate an example.

In this new set, all fuel models with an herbaceous component are dynamic. In a dynamic fuel model, live herbaceous load is transferred to dead as a function of the live herbaceous moisture content. Although the new fuel model parameters can be input to a nondynamic fire behavior processor, that approach does not produce the intended result. Using the dynamic fuel models in a nondynamic fire behavior model would leave the live herbaceous load in the live category, regardless of moisture content. The grass models will therefore predict no (or very little) spread and intensity under any wind or moisture condition. The change to dynamic fuel models is really a change in both the fire behavior processors and, concurrently, how fuel models for grass- or herbaceous-dominated fuelbeds are conceived. In this case, our desire for grass and herbaceous fuel models that could be used at various levels of curing precipitated the change in fire behavior processors.

Fire behavior modeling systems must be modified in order to use the new dynamic fuel models correctly. Check the documentation of each fire behavior processor to be sure it implements the dynamic fuel models as intended.

Naming Convention

Fuel models in the new set are grouped by fire-carrying fuel type. The number of fuel models within each fuel type varies. Each fuel type has been assigned a mnemonic two-letter code. Nonburnable fuel models, even though not really a "fuel," were included in the set to facilitate consistent mapping of these areas on a fuel model map. Fuel types were ordered in a way similar to the original 13, with hybrid fuel types (such as Timber-Understory) generally between the two types that compose the hybrid. Fuel types are as follows:

- (NB) Nonburnable
- (GR) Grass
- (GS) Grass-Shrub
- (SH) Shrub
- (TU) Timber-Understory

- (TL) Timber Litter
- (SB) Slash-Blowdown

To facilitate both communication and computation, we use a three-part fuel model reference scheme:

- Fuel model number (between 1 and 256; for use in computer code and mapping applications)
- Fuel model code (three digits; used for oral and written communication and input to fire modeling systems)
- Fuel model name (any length string of characters; used for description and long-hand written communication)

For example:

number	code	name
101	GR1	Short, sparse, dry climate grass

Within a fuel type, fuel models are ordered by increasing heat per unit area (at 8 percent dead, 75 percent live fuel moisture content). Wind speed and slope steepness do not affect heat per unit area. Fuel model numbers were kept below 256 so that an eight-bit number could be used for storing fuel model information in mapping or database applications.

Each fuel type has been assigned a block of fuel model numbers (table 1) so that fuel model maps colored by fuel type are simple to create. For example, a coarse-scale map (for which identifying a specific fuel model is not required) can be colored such that all fuel model numbers in a block (representing a fuel type) are the same color. Only a portion of each block is used by the new fuel model set. The unused fuel model numbers are reserved for future standard fuel models and for custom fuel models. This allows future standard and custom fuel models to be in the correct fuel type number block.

The dead fuel extinction moisture assigned to the fuel model defines the weighted-average dead fuel moisture content at which the fire will no longer spread in the Rothermel model. This modeling parameter is generally associated with climate (humid versus dry), though fire science research has yet to explain the mechanism for the association. Fuel models for dry climates tend to have lower dead fuel moistures of extinction, while fuel models for humid-climate areas tend to have higher moistures of extinction. Fuel model names (and the fuel model selection guide) include reference to the general climate where the fuel model is found.

Table 1—Assignment of current fuel model numbers to standard and custom fuel models.

Fuel type	Fuel model number block	Used in original or new set	Reserved for future standard fuel models	Available for custom fuel models
	1-13	1-13		
	14-89			14-89
NB	90-99	91-93, 98-99[a]	94-95	90, 96-97
GR	100-119	101-109	110-112	100, 113-119
GS	120-139	121-124	125-130	120, 131-139
SH	140-159	141-149	150-152	140, 153-159
TU	160-179	161-165	166-170	160, 171-179
TL	180-199	181-189	190-192	180, 193-199
SB	200-219	201-204	205-210	200, 211-219
	220-256			220-256

[a] The gap in the NB numbering sequence is to retain fuel model numbers 98 as open water and 99 as "rock" (bare ground), as has been convention in FARSITE.

Dynamic Fuel Models

In this new set, all fuel models that have a live herbaceous component are "dynamic," meaning that their herbaceous load shifts between live and dead depending on the specified live herbaceous moisture content. In the Fuel Models section, refer to the model parameters list ("fuel model type" column) to see which models contain live herbaceous load and are therefore dynamic.

The dynamic fuel model process is described by Burgan (1979); the method is outlined and outlined below, with graphic presentation in figure 1.

- If live herbaceous moisture content is 120 percent or higher, the herbaceous fuels are green, and all herbaceous load stays in the live category at the given moisture content.
- If live herbaceous moisture content is 30 percent or lower, the herbaceous fuels are considered fully cured, and all herbaceous load is transferred to dead herbaceous.
- If live herbaceous moisture content is between 30 and 120 percent, then part of the herb load is transferred to dead. For example, if live herb moisture content is 75 percent (halfway between 30 and 120 percent), then half of the herbaceous load is transferred to dead herbaceous, the remainder stays in the live herbaceous class.

Load transferred to dead is not simply placed in the dead 1-hr timelag class. Instead a new dead herbaceous class is created so that the surface-area-to-volume ratio of the live herbaceous component is preserved. However, for simplicity the moisture content of the new dead herbaceous category is set to the same as that for the dead 1-hr timelag class.

When evaluating dynamic models, be aware that live herbaceous moisture content significantly affects fire behavior because herbaceous load shifts between live and dead, and dead fuel usually has much lower moisture content than live. It will often be preferable to estimate live herbaceous moisture content by working backward from observed or estimated degree of herbaceous curing (table 2). For example, if the fuelbed is observed to be 50 percent cured, use a value of 75 percent for live herbaceous moisture content.

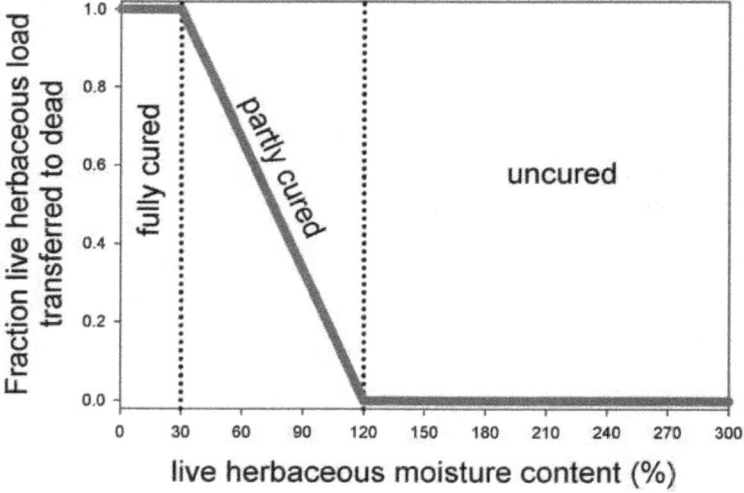

Figure 1—Graphical representation of the dynamic fuel model process.

6

USDA Forest Service Gen. Tech. Rep. RMRS-GTR-153. 2005

Table 2—Level of curing versus live herbaceous moisture content.

Level of curing		Live herbaceous moisture content
Uncured	0 percent	120 percent or more
One-quarter	25	98
One-third	33	90
One-half	50	75
Two-thirds	66	60
Three-quarters	75	53
Fully cured	100	30 or less

None of the original 13 fire behavior fuel models is dynamic. Therefore, direct comparisons between the new and original fuel models can only be made if the live herbaceous moisture content is 30 percent (fully cured) or lower. For example, models GR6 and GR8 are similar to original fuel model 3, but their behavior over a range of live herbaceous moisture content is very different (fig. 2). Fuel model 3 does not have a live herbaceous component, so its behavior does not change as that input is varied. Fuel models GR6 and GR8 are both dynamic, so fire behavior decreases rapidly with higher levels of live fuel moisture (less curing).

To preserve the static nature of original fuel model 2 (which contains live herbaceous load as well as dead grass) and to preserve the ability to create custom fuel models in which dynamic load transfer does not take place, the fuel model description includes a fuel model type. A static fuel model with live herbaceous load should keep that load in the live category regardless of moisture content, whereas the same fuel model would undergo the load transfer if its type is dynamic. Custom fuel models can be either static or dynamic. If a fuel model does not have load in the live herbaceous category, then the fuel model type is irrelevant.

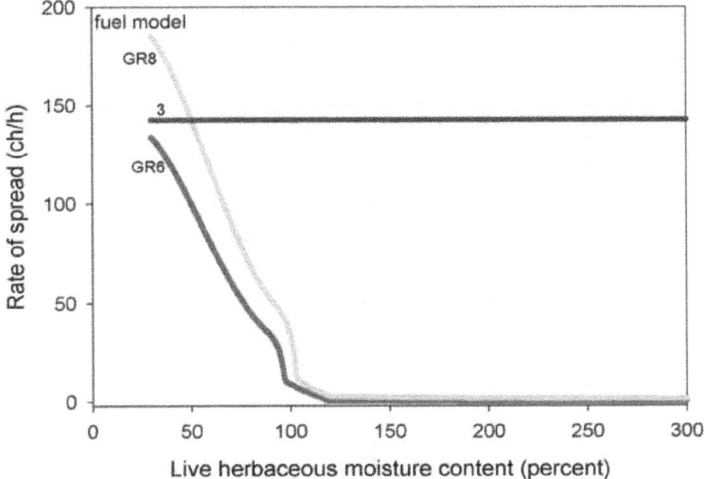

Figure 2—Comparison of dynamic fuel models GR6 and GR8 with static fuel model 3.

USDA Forest Service Gen. Tech. Rep. RMRS-GTR-153. 2005

7

Moisture Scenarios

To facilitate standard comparisons of the new fire behavior fuel models with the original 13 fuel models and with each other, we developed standard dead (table 3) and live (table 4) fuel moisture scenarios. Separate live and dead scenarios were needed so that live and dead fuels could vary independently. There are 16 unique moisture scenario combinations. However, fire behavior predicted with fuel models without a live fuel component is not affected by the live moisture scenario. Live moisture scenarios cover a range of live herbaceous moisture corresponding to fully cured (30 percent) to uncured (fully green; 120 percent).

Table 3—Dead fuel moisture content values (percent) for the dead fuel moisture scenarios.

	D1 Very low	D2 Low	D3 Moderate	D4 High
1-hr	3	6	9	12
10-hr	4	7	10	13
100-hr	5	8	11	14

Table 4—Live fuel moisture content values (percent) for the live fuel moisture scenarios.

	L1 Fully cured Very low	L2 Two-thirds cured Low	L3 One-third cured Moderate	L4 Fully green (uncured) High
Live herbaceous	30	60	90	120
Live woody	60	90	120	150

Fuel Model Selection

This document contains two aids to fuel model selection: a fuel model selection guide and a set of crosswalks. Use the crosswalks if you have an area already designated as one of the 13 original fuel models and you want guidance on selecting one of the new models for that area. Use the fuel model selection guide for assistance in selecting a fuel model from knowledge of general fuelbed properties.

Both the selection guide and crosswalks offer suggestions to consider, not conclusive results. The final fuel model selection must be made by the user based on experience with fire behavior in the fuelbed under consideration.

Fuel Model Selection Guide

To select a fuel model:

1.   Determine the general fire-carrying fuel type: grass, grass-shrub, shrub, timber litter, timber with (grass or shrub) understory, or slash or blowdown fuels. Estimate which stratum of surface fuels is most likely to carry the fire. For example, the fire may be in a forested area, but if the forest canopy is open, grass, not needle litter, might carry the fire. In this case a grass model should be considered.

2.   The dead fuel extinction moisture assigned to the fuel model defines the moisture content of dead fuels at which the fire will no longer spread. This fuel parameter, unique to the Rothermel surface fire spread model, is generally associated with climate (humid versus dry). That is, fuel models for dry areas tend to have lower dead fuel moistures of extinction, while fuel models for wet humid areas tend to have higher moistures of extinction.

3.   Note the general depth, compactness, and size of the fuel, and the relative amount of live vegetation.

4.   Do not restrict your selection by fuel model name or fuel type. After selecting a fuel model, view its predicted fire behavior to be sure the predicted behavior agrees with your expectation or observation.

In this guide we refer to spread rates and flame lengths as being very low, low, moderate, high, very high, and extreme—assuming two-thirds cured herbaceous, dry dead fuels (moisture scenario D2L2), a midflame wind speed of 5 mi/h, and zero slope (table 5).

Table 5—Adjective class definitions for predicted fire behavior.

Adjective class	ROS (ch/h)	FL (ft)
Very Low	0-2	0-1
Low	2-5	1-4
Moderate	5-20	4-8
High	20-50	8-12
Very High	50-150	12-25
Extreme	>150	>25

The general fire-carrying fuel type is:

1. **Nearly pure grass and/or forb type (Grass)**
   a. Arid to semiarid climate (rainfall deficient in summer). Extinction moisture content is 15 percent.
      i. **GR1** Grass is short, patchy, and possibly heavily grazed. Spread rate moderate; flame length low.
      ii. **GR2** Moderately coarse continuous grass, average depth about 1 foot. Spread rate high; flame length moderate.
      iii. **GR4** Moderately coarse continuous grass, average depth about 2 feet. Spread rate very high; flame length high.
      iv. **GR7** Moderately coarse continuous grass, average depth about 3 feet. Spread rate very high; flame length very high.
   b. Subhumid to humid climate (rainfall adequate in all seasons). Extinction moisture content is 30 to 40 percent.
      i. **GR1** Grass is short, patchy, and possibly heavily grazed. Spread rate moderate; flame length low.
      ii. **GR3** Very coarse grass, average depth about 2 feet. Spread rate high; flame length moderate.
      iii. **GR5** Dense, coarse grass, average depth about 1 to 2 feet. Spread rate very high; flame length high.
      iv. **GR6** Dryland grass about 1 to 2 feet tall. Spread rate very high; flame length very high.
      v. **GR8** Heavy, coarse, continuous grass 3 to 5 feet tall. Spread rate very high; flame length very high.
      vi. **GR9** Very heavy, coarse, continuous grass 5 to 8 feet tall. Spread rate extreme; flame length extreme.

2. **Mixture of grass and shrub, up to about 50 percent shrub coverage (Grass-Shrub)**
   a. Arid to semiarid climate (rainfall deficient in summer). Extinction moisture content is 15 percent.
      i. **GS1** Shrubs are about 1 foot high, low grass load. Spread rate moderate; flame length low.
      ii. **GS2** Shrubs are 1 to 3 feet high, moderate grass load. Spread rate high; flame length moderate.
   b. Subhumid to humid climate (rainfall adequate in all seasons). Extinction moisture content is 30 to 40 percent.
      i. **GS3** Moderate grass/shrub load, average grass/shrub depth less than 2 feet. Spread rate high; flame length moderate.
      ii. **GS4** Heavy grass/shrub load, depth greater than 2 feet. Spread rate high; flame length very high.

3. **Shrubs cover at least 50 percent of the site; grass sparse to nonexistent (Shrub)**
   a. Arid to semiarid climate (rainfall deficient in summer). Extinction moisture content is 15 percent.
      i. **SH1** Low shrub fuel load, fuelbed depth about 1 foot; some grass may be present. Spread rate very low; flame length very low.
      ii. **SH2** Moderate fuel load (higher than SH1), depth about 1 foot, no grass fuel present. Spread rate low; flame length low.
      iii. **SH5** Heavy shrub load, depth 4 to 6 feet. Spread rate very high; flame length very high.

    iv. **SH7** Very heavy shrub load, depth 4 to 6 feet. Spread rate lower than SH5, but flame length similar. Spread rate high; flame length very high.

  b. Subhumid to humid climate (rainfall adequate in all seasons). Extinction moisture content is 30 to 40 percent.

    i. **SH3** Moderate shrub load, possibly with pine overstory or herbaceous fuel, fuel bed depth 2 to 3 feet. Spread rate low; flame length low.

    ii. **SH4** Low to moderate shrub and litter load, possibly with pine overstory, fuel bed depth about 3 feet. Spread rate high; flame length moderate.

    iii. **SH6** Dense shrubs, little or no herb fuel, depth about 2 feet. Spread rate high; flame length high.

    iv. **SH8** Dense shrubs, little or no herb fuel, depth about 3 feet. Spread rates high; flame length high.

    v. **SH9** Dense, finely branched shrubs with significant fine dead fuel, about 4 to 6 feet tall; some herbaceous fuel may be present. Spread rate high, flame length very high.

4. Grass or shrubs mixed with litter from forest canopy (Timber-Understory)

  a. Semiarid to subhumid climate. Extinction moisture content is 20 percent.

    i. **TU1** Fuelbed is low load of grass and/or shrub with litter. Spread rate low; flame length low.

    ii. **TU4** Fuelbed is short conifer trees with grass or moss understory. Spread rate moderate; flame length moderate.

    iii. **TU5** Fuelbed is high load conifer litter with shrub understory. Spread rate moderate; flame length moderate.

  b. Humid climate. Extinction moisture content is 30 percent.

    i. **TU2** Fuelbed is moderate litter load with shrub component. Spread rate moderate; flame length low.

    ii. **TU3** Fuelbed is moderate litter load with grass and shrub components. Spread rate high; flame length moderate.

5. Dead and down woody fuel (litter) beneath a forest canopy (Timber Litter)

  a. Fuelbed is recently burned but able to carry wildland fire.

    i. **TL1** Light to moderate load, fuels 1 to 2 inches deep. Spread rate very low; flame length very low.

  b. Fuelbed not recently burned.

    i. Fuelbed composed of broadleaf (hardwood) litter.

      1. **TL2** Low load, compact. Spread rate very low; flame length very low.

      2. **TL6** Moderate load, less compact. Spread rate moderate; flame length low.

      3. **TL9** Very high load, fluffy. Spread rate moderate; flame length moderate.

    ii. Fuelbed composed of long-needle pine litter.

      1. **TL8** moderate load and compactness may include small amount of herbaceous load. Spread rate moderate; flame length low.

    iii. Fuelbed not composed broadleaf or long-needle pine litter.

      1. Fuelbed includes both fine and coarse fuels.

        a. **TL4** Moderate load, includes small diameter downed logs. Spread rate low; flame length low.

        b. **TL7** Heavy load, includes larger diameter downed logs. Spread rate low; flame length low.

      2. Fuelbed does not include coarse fuels.

        a. **TL3** Moderate load conifer litter. Spread rate very low; flame length low.

  b. **TL5** High load conifer litter; light slash or mortality fuel. Spread rate low; flame length low.

  c. **TL9** Very high load broadleaf litter; heavy needle-drape in otherwise sparse shrub layer. Spread rate moderate; flame length moderate.

6. **Activity fuel (slash) or debris from wind damage (blowdown) (Slash-Blowdown)**
  a. Fuelbed is activity fuel.
   i. **SB1** Fine fuel load is 10 to 20 tons/acre, weighted toward fuels 1 to 3 inches diameter class, depth is less than 1 foot. Spread rate moderate; flame length low.
   ii. **SB2** Fine fuel load is 7 to 12 tons/acre, evenly distributed across 0 to 0.25, 0.25 to 1, and 1 to 3 inch diameter classes, depth is about 1 foot. Spread rate moderate; flame length moderate.
   iii. **SB3** Fine fuel load is 7 to 12 tons/acre, weighted toward 0 to 0.25 inch diameter class, depth is more than 1 foot. Spread rate high; flame length high.
  b. Fuelbed is blowdown.
   i. **SB2** Blowdown is scattered, with many trees still standing. Spread rate moderate; flame length moderate.
   ii. **SB3** Blowdown is moderate, trees compacted to near the ground. Spread rate high; flame length high.
   iii. **SB4** Blowdown is total, fuelbed not compacted, foliage still attached. Spread rate very high; flame length very high.

7. **Insufficient wildland fuel to carry wildland fire under any condition (Nonburnable)**
  a. **NB1** Urban or suburban development; insufficient wildland fuel to carry wildland fire.
  b. **NB2** Snow/ice.
  c. **NB3** Agricultural field, maintained in nonburnable condition.
  d. **NB8** Open water.
  e. **NB9** Bare ground.

Fuel Model Crosswalks

These crosswalks will help users of the original 13 fuel models make the transition to using the new set. For each of the 13 original fuel models we suggest one or more fuel models from the new set to consider. However, you are not limited to these choices; always use the fuel model that provides the best fit for fire behavior prediction.

The crosswalks use adjective classes to compare spread rate and flame length between the original fuel models and their related models from the new set (table 6).

Note: We computed the relative change in fire behavior between original and new models using 5 miles/hour midflame wind speed, low dead fuel moisture, two-thirds cured herbaceous fuels, and low live woody fuels (moisture scenario D2L2). Relative change among fuel models might be different for different environmental conditions; use these crosswalks as a guide only.

There is a crosswalk table for each major fire-carrying fuel type of the original 13 fuel models. The crosswalk uses adjective classes to compare spread rate and flame length between the original 13 fuel models and their related models from the new set.

Table 6—Adjective class definitions for fire behavior comparisons.

Adjective class	Relative change in fire behavior (percent change from original model)
Comparable	0-15
Slightly higher/lower	15-50
Higher/lower	50-100
Much higher/lower	100-200
Significantly higher/lower	200+

Grass fuel type

Consider using one of these fuel models from the new set...	... if you used one of these models from the original set.		
	1 Short Grass	2 Timber Grass and Understory	3 Tall Grass
GR1	For very sparse or heavily grazed grass; for lower spread rate and flame length		
GR2	For slightly lower spread rate and comparable flame length	For comparable spread rate and slightly lower flame length	
GR3			For lower spread rate and slightly lower flame length
GR4	For slightly lower spread rate and much higher flame length	For higher spread rate and slightly higher flame length	
GR5			For lower spread rate and slightly lower flame length
GR6			For slightly lower spread rate and comparable flame length
GR7	For comparable spread rate and significantly higher flame length	For much higher spread rate and flame length	For comparable spread rate and slightly higher flame length
GR8			For comparable spread rate and higher flame length
GR9			For higher spread rate and much higher flame length
GS1		For slightly lower spread rate and lower flame length	
GS2		For slightly lower spread rate and flame length	

Note: All grass fuel models from the new set are dynamic fuel models, which means that herbaceous load is transferred between live and dead categories according to live herbaceous moisture content. Original models 1 and 3 have only a dead component. Original fuel model 2 has a live herbaceous component but is static. Exact fire behavior comparisons between original and new grass models can only be made when live herbaceous moisture content is 30 percent or less. These comparisons were made with a live herbaceous moisture content of 60 percent (two-thirds cured).

Shrub fuel type

Consider using one of these fuel models from the new set...	...if you used one of these models from the original set.			
	4 Chaparral	**5** Brush	**6** Dormant Brush	**7** Southern Rough
SH1		For lower spread rate and flame length	For lower spread rate and flame length	
SH2		For lower spread rate and slightly lower flame length	For lower spread rate and flame length	
SH3				For lower spread rate and flame length
SH4			For slightly lower spread rate and comparable flame length	For comparable spread rate and flame length
SH5	For slightly lower spread rate and flame length	For much higher spread rate and flame length		
SH6			For slightly lower spreadrate and higher flame length	For slightly lower spread rate and higher flame length
SH7	For slightly lower spread rate and flame length	For slightly higher spread rate and much higher flame length		
SH8				For slightly lower spread rate and higher flame length
SH9				For slightly higher spread rate and much higher flame length
TU5		For lower spread rate and slightly higher flame length		
GS2		For comparable spread rate and slightly lower flame length; with grass component		

Timber fuel type

Consider using one of these fuel models from the new set...	... if you used one of these models from the original set.		
	8 **Compact Timber Litter**	**9** **Hardwood Litter**	**10** **Timber (Understory)**
TL1	For lower spread rate and slightly lower flame length		
TL2		For lower spread rate and flame length	
TL3	For comparable spread rate and flame length		
TL4	For slightly higher spread rate and flame length		
TL5	For much higher spread rate and higher flame length		
TL6		For slightly lower spread rate and comparable flame length	
TL7	For slightly higher spread rate and higher flame length		
TL8		For slightly lower spread rate and slightly higher flame length	
TL9		For comparable spread rate and higher flame length	
TU1	For higher spread rate and flame length		For lower spread rate and flame length
TU2			For slightly higher spread rate and slightly lower flame length; high extinction moisture
TU3			For much higher spread rate and slightly higher flame length; high extinction moisture
TU4			For slightly higher spread rate and comparable flame length
TU5			For comparable spread rate and slightly higher flame length
SH2			For lower spread rate and flame length

JSDA Forest Service Gen. Tech. Rep. RMRS-GTR-153. 2005

15

Slash fuel type

Consider using one of these fuel models from the new set...	... if you used one of these models from the original set.		
	11 Light Logging Slash	12 Medium Logging Slash	13 Heavy Logging Slash
TL5	For slightly lower spread rate and flame length		
SB1	For comparable spread rate and flame length	For lower spread rate and flame length	
SB2	For much higher spread rate and higher flame length	For comparable spread rate and slightly lower flame length	For comparable spread rate and slightly lower flame length
SB3		For much higher spread rate and comparable flame length	For higher spread rate and comparable flame length
SB4			For significantly higher spread rate and slightly higher flame length

Fuel Models

In this section we list the fuel model parameters and describe each fuel model and fuel type.

Fuel Model Parameters

Parameters of the new fuel models include load by class and component, surface-area-to-volume (SAV) ratio by class and component, fuel model type (static or dynamic), fuelbed depth, extinction moisture content, and fuel particle heat content (table 7). Fuel inputs not listed are constant for the entire set: 10-hr dead fuel SAV ratio is 109 1/ft, and 100-hr SAV ratio is 30 1/ft. Total fuel particle mineral content is 5.55 percent; effective (silica-free) mineral content is 1.00 percent. Ovendry fuel particle density is 32 lb/ft^3.

Fuel Type Page

A fuel type page consists of a brief description of the fuel type followed by a pair of charts depicting predicted fire behavior over a range of midflame wind speeds, one for headfire spread rate and one for headfire flame length. These charts are for moisture scenario D2L2 (low dead fuel moisture, two-thirds cured live herbaceous, low live woody fuel moisture). The moisture contents by class and category are:

Dead 1-hr	6 percent
Dead 10-hr	7
Dead 100-hr	8
Live herbaceous	60 (2/3 cured)
Live woody	90

Use the charts to compare the relative behavior of the various models within a fuel type, but be aware that the relative behavior may be different at other moisture contents.

Fuel models with herbaceous load are sensitive to live herbaceous moisture content. The herbaceous fuel in moisture scenario D2L2 is two-thirds cured, which means that 67 percent of the herbaceous load is actually at the dead 1-hr moisture content, while the remaining 33 percent retains the 60 percent moisture content.

USDA Forest Service Gen. Tech. Rep. RMRS-GTR-153. 2005

17

Table 7—Fuel model parameters.

Fuel model code	Fuel load (t/ac)					Fuel model type[a]	SAV ratio (1/ft)[b]			Fuel bed depth (ft)	Dead fuel extinction moisture (percent)	Heat content BTU/lb)[c]
	1-hr	10-hr	100-hr	Live herb	Live woody		Dead 1-hr	Live herb	Live woody			
GR1	0.10	0.00	0.00	0.30	0.00	dynamic	2200	2000	9999	0.4	15	8000
GR2	0.10	0.00	0.00	1.00	0.00	dynamic	2000	1800	9999	1.0	15	8000
GR3	0.10	0.40	0.00	1.50	0.00	dynamic	1500	1300	9999	2.0	30	8000
GR4	0.25	0.00	0.00	1.90	0.00	dynamic	2000	1800	9999	2.0	15	8000
GR5	0.40	0.00	0.00	2.50	0.00	dynamic	1800	1600	9999	1.5	40	8000
GR6	0.10	0.00	0.00	3.40	0.00	dynamic	2200	2000	9999	1.5	40	9000
GR7	1.00	0.00	0.00	5.40	0.00	dynamic	2000	1800	9999	3.0	15	8000
GR8	0.50	1.00	0.00	7.30	0.00	dynamic	1500	1300	9999	4.0	30	8000
GR9	1.00	1.00	0.00	9.00	0.00	dynamic	1800	1600	9999	5.0	40	8000
GS1	0.20	0.00	0.00	0.50	0.65	dynamic	2000	1800	1800	0.9	15	8000
GS2	0.50	0.50	0.00	0.60	1.00	dynamic	2000	1800	1800	1.5	15	8000
GS3	0.30	0.25	0.00	1.45	1.25	dynamic	1800	1600	1600	1.8	40	8000
GS4	1.90	0.30	0.10	3.40	7.10	dynamic	1800	1600	1600	2.1	40	8000
SH1	0.25	0.25	0.00	0.15	1.30	dynamic	2000	1800	1600	1.0	15	8000
SH2	1.35	2.40	0.75	0.00	3.85	N/A	2000	9999	1600	1.0	15	8000
SH3	0.45	3.00	0.00	0.00	6.20	N/A	1600	9999	1400	2.4	40	8000
SH4	0.85	1.15	0.20	0.00	2.55	N/A	2000	1800	1600	3.0	30	8000
SH5	3.60	2.10	0.00	0.00	2.90	N/A	750	9999	1600	6.0	15	8000
SH6	2.90	1.45	0.00	0.00	1.40	N/A	750	9999	1600	2.0	30	8000
SH7	3.50	5.30	2.20	0.00	3.40	N/A	750	9999	1600	6.0	15	8000
SH8	2.05	3.40	0.85	0.00	4.35	N/A	750	9999	1600	3.0	40	8000
SH9	4.50	2.45	0.00	1.55	7.00	dynamic	750	1800	1500	4.4	40	8000
TU1	0.20	0.90	1.50	0.20	0.90	dynamic	2000	1800	1600	0.6	20	8000
TU2	0.95	1.80	1.25	0.00	0.20	N/A	2000	9999	1600	1.0	30	8000
TU3	1.10	0.15	0.25	0.65	1.10	dynamic	1800	1600	1400	1.3	30	8000
TU4	4.50	0.00	0.00	0.00	2.00	N/A	2300	9999	2000	0.5	12	8000
TU5	4.00	4.00	3.00	0.00	3.00	N/A	1500	9999	750	1.0	25	8000
TL1	1.00	2.20	3.60	0.00	0.00	N/A	2000	9999	9999	0.2	30	8000
TL2	1.40	2.30	2.20	0.00	0.00	N/A	2000	9999	9999	0.2	25	8000
TL3	0.50	2.20	2.80	0.00	0.00	N/A	2000	9999	9999	0.3	20	8000
TL4	0.50	1.50	4.20	0.00	0.00	N/A	2000	9999	9999	0.4	25	8000
TL5	1.15	2.50	4.40	0.00	0.00	N/A	2000	9999	1600	0.6	25	8000
TL6	2.40	1.20	1.20	0.00	0.00	N/A	2000	9999	9999	0.3	25	8000
TL7	0.30	1.40	8.10	0.00	0.00	N/A	2000	9999	9999	0.4	25	8000
TL8	5.80	1.40	1.10	0.00	0.00	N/A	1800	9999	9999	0.3	35	8000
TL9	6.65	3.30	4.15	0.00	0.00	N/A	1800	9999	1600	0.6	35	8000
SB1	1.50	3.00	11.00	0.00	0.00	N/A	2000	9999	9999	1.0	25	8000
SB2	4.50	4.25	4.00	0.00	0.00	N/A	2000	9999	9999	1.0	25	8000
SB3	5.50	2.75	3.00	0.00	0.00	N/A	2000	9999	9999	1.2	25	8000
SB4	5.25	3.50	5.25	0.00	0.00	N/A	2000	9999	9999	2.7	25	8000

[a] Fuel model type does not apply to fuel models without live herbaceous load.
[b] The value 9999 was assigned in cases where there is no load in a particular fuel class or category
[c] The same heat content value was applied to both live and dead fuel categories.

Fuel Model Page

A fuel model page consists of:

- The three-part fuel model naming
- A set of three photos
- A brief description of the fuel model
- A summary of computed fuel model characteristics
- A pair of charts depicting fire behavior over a range of midflame wind speeds

Further details follow.

Naming—The fuel model code and number (in parentheses) are displayed on the first line, followed on the next line by the full fuel model name. The fuel model code is used for oral and written communication and for input to fire behavior models. The fuel model number is used internally by some fire behavior models and for mapping applications. The fuel model name is a brief description of the fuel model.

Photos—Up to three representative photos were selected to illustrate each fuel model. Conditions other than those illustrated may still be appropriate for the fuel model; use the photos as a general guide only.

Description—Main characteristics of each fuel model are briefly described.

Summary characteristics—Summary characteristics of each fuel model include fine fuel load, characteristic surface-area-to-volume ratio (SAV), packing ratio, and extinction moisture content.

Fine fuel load is defined as the dead 1-hr load plus the live herbaceous and live woody loads. Across the new set of 40 fuel models, fine fuel load ranges from 0.30 to 13.05 tons/acre.

Characteristic SAV is the average SAV across all fuel classes and categories, weighted by the surface area within each class and category. Characteristic SAV ranges from 1,144 to 2,216 1/ft in this new set of fuel models.

Packing ratio is the fraction of fuelbed volume that is occupied by fuel particles, a function of fuel load, fuelbed depth, and fuel particle density. In this fuel model set, packing ratio varies from 0.00143 to 0.04878 (dimensionless).

Extinction moisture content is the weighted average dead fuel moisture content at which the fire spread model predicts spread will not take place. More important, the amount by which the extinction moisture content exceeds the actual determines (in part) fire behavior. Thus, for a given dead fuel moisture content, predicted fire spread increases with increasing extinction moisture content.

Fire behavior charts—A pair of charts depicts predicted fire behavior (spread rate and flame length) for each fuel model over a range of midflame wind speeds. All predictions use live moisture scenario L2 (60 percent live herbaceous moisture content, 90 percent live woody), which corresponds to a two-thirds cured herbaceous fuelbed. The four lines on each chart refer to dead fuel moisture scenarios (table 3).

Nonburnable Fuel Type Models (NB)

The nonburnable "fuel models" are included on the next five pages to provide consistency in how the nonburnable portions of the landscape are displayed on a fuel model map. In all NB fuel models there is no fuel load—wildland fire will not spread.

USDA Forest Service Gen. Tech. Rep. RMRS-GTR-153. 2005

19

NB1 (91)

Urban/Developed

Description: Fuel model NB1 consists of land covered by urban and suburban development. To be called NB1, the area under consideration must not support wildland fire spread. In some cases, areas mapped as NB1 may experience structural fire losses during a wildland fire incident; however, structure ignition in those cases is either house to house or by firebrands, neither of which is directly modeled using fire behavior fuel models. If sufficient fuel vegetation surrounds structures such that wildland fire spread is possible, then choose a fuel model appropriate for the wildland vegetation rather than NB1.

Expected fire behavior:

No fire spread

NB2 (92)

Snow/Ice

Description: Land covered by permanent snow or ice is included in NB2. Areas covered by seasonal snow can be mapped to two different fuel models: NB2 for use when snow covered and another for use in the fire season.

Expected fire behavior:

No fire spread

USDA Forest Service Gen. Tech. Rep. RMRS-GTR-153. 2005

21

NB3 (93)

Agricultural

Description: Fuel model NB3 is agricultural land maintained in a nonburnable condition; examples include irrigated annual crops, mowed or tilled orchards, and so forth. However, there are many agricultural areas that are not kept in a nonburnable condition. For example, grass is often allowed to grow beneath vines or orchard trees, and wheat or similar crops are allowed to cure before harvest; in those cases use a fuel model other than NB3.

Expected fire behavior:

No fire spread

NB8 (98)

Open Water

Description: Land covered by open bodies of water such as lakes, rivers and oceans comprises NB8.

Expected fire behavior:

No fire spread

NB9 (99)

Bare Ground

Description: Land devoid of enough fuel to support wildland fire spread is covered by fuel model NB9. Such areas may include gravel pits, arid deserts with little vegetation, sand dunes, rock outcroppings, beaches, and so forth.

Expected fire behavior:

No fire spread

Grass Fuel Type Models (GR)

The primary carrier of fire in the GR fuel models is grass. Grass fuels can vary from heavily grazed grass stubble or sparse natural grass to dense grass more than 6 feet tall. Fire behavior varies from moderate spread rate and low flame length in the sparse grass to extreme spread rate and flame length in the tall grass models.

All GR fuel models are dynamic, meaning that their live herbaceous fuel load shifts from live to dead as a function of live herbaceous moisture content. The effect of live herbaceous moisture content on spread rate and intensity is strong.

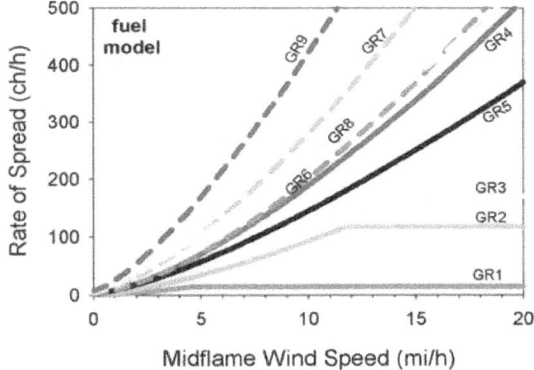

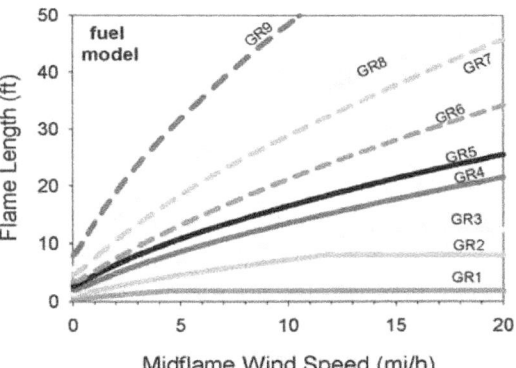

USDA Forest Service Gen. Tech. Rep. RMRS-GTR-153. 2005

25

GR1 (101)

Short, Sparse Dry Climate Grass (Dynamic)

Description: The primary carrier of fire in GR1 is sparse grass, though small amounts of fine dead fuel may be present. The grass in GR1 is generally short, either naturally or by grazing, and may be sparse or discontinuous. The moisture of extinction of GR1 is indicative of a dry climate fuelbed, but GR1 may also be applied in high extinction moisture fuelbeds because in both cases predicted spread rate and flame length are low compared to other GR models.

Fine fuel load (t/ac)	0.40
Characteristic SAV (ft 1)	2054
Packing ratio (dimensionless)	0.00143
Extinction moisture content (percent)	15

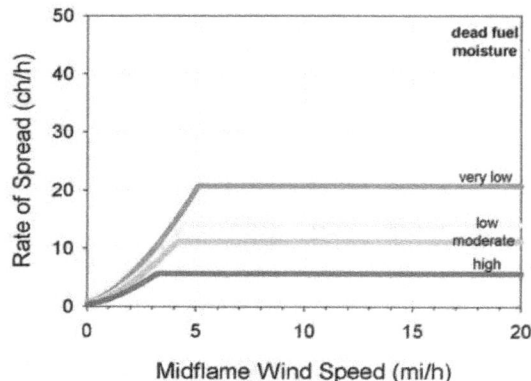   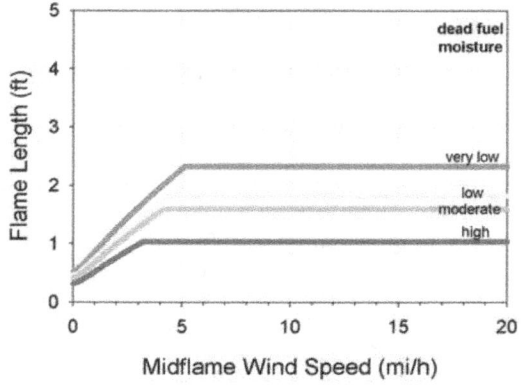

26

USDA Forest Service Gen. Tech. Rep. RMRS-GTR-153. 2005

GR2 (102)

Low Load, Dry Climate Grass (Dynamic)

Description: The primary carrier of fire in GR2 is grass, though small amounts of fine dead fuel may be present. Load is greater than GR1, and fuelbed may be more continuous. Shrubs, if present, do not affect fire behavior.

Fine fuel load (t/ac)	1.10
Characteristic SAV (ft 1)	1820
Packing ratio (dimensionless)	0.00158
Extinction moisture content (percent)	15

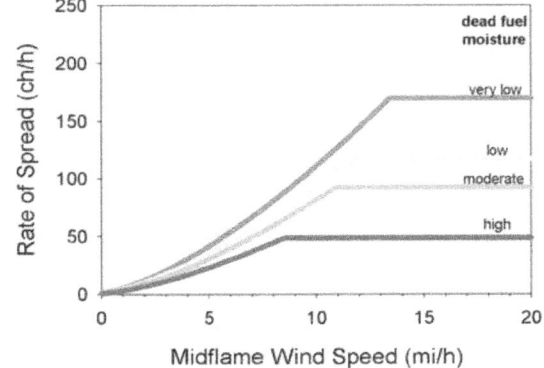 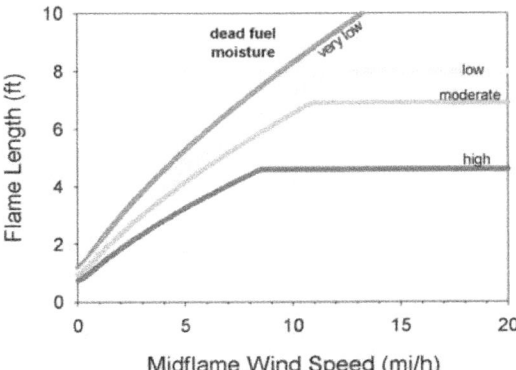

USDA Forest Service Gen. Tech. Rep. RMRS-GTR-153. 2005

27

GR3 (103)

Low Load, Very Coarse, Humid Climate Grass (Dynamic)

Description: The primary carrier of fire in GR3 is continuous, coarse, humid climate grass. Grass and herb fuel load is relatively light; fuelbed depth is about 2 feet. Shrubs are not present in significant quantity to affect fire behavior.

Fine fuel load (t/ac)	1.60
Characteristic SAV (ft 1)	1290
Packing ratio (dimensionless)	0.00143
Extinction moisture content (percent)	30

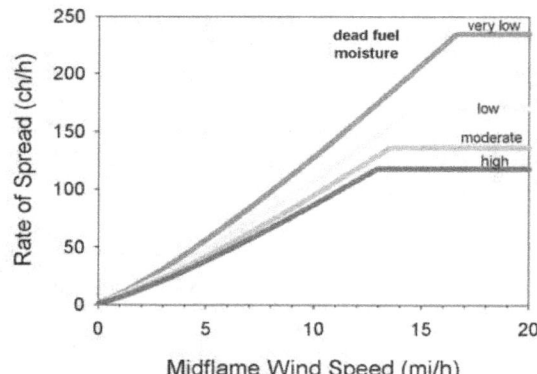 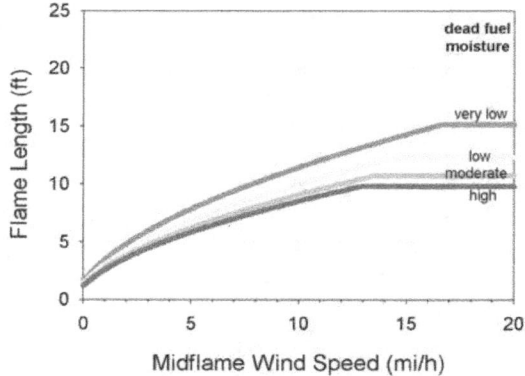

28

USDA Forest Service Gen. Tech. Rep. RMRS-GTR-153. 2005

GR4 (104)

Moderate Load, Dry Climate Grass (Dynamic)

Description: The primary carrier of fire in GR4 is continuous, dry climate grass.

Load and depth are greater than GR2; fuelbed depth is about 2 feet.

Fine fuel load (t/ac)	2.15
Characteristic SAV (ft 1)	1826
Packing ratio (dimensionless)	0.00154
Extinction moisture content (percent)	15

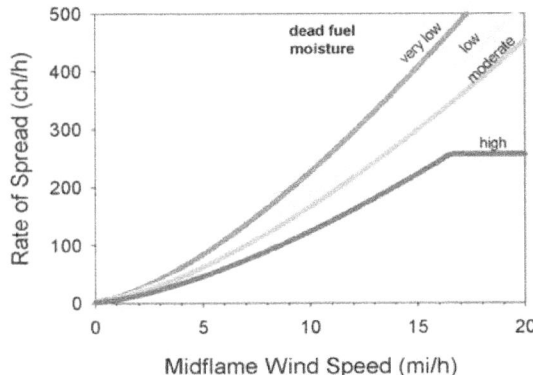 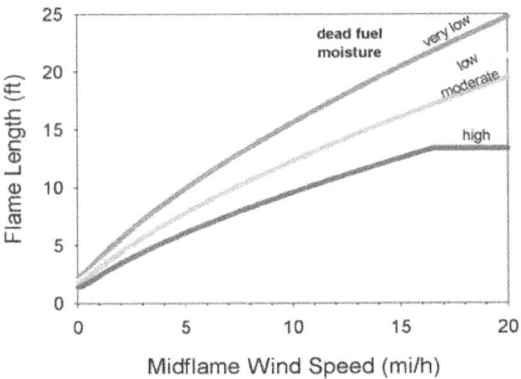

JSDA Forest Service Gen. Tech. Rep. RMRS-GTR-153. 2005

29

GR5 (105)

Low Load, Humid Climate Grass (Dynamic)

Description: The primary carrier of fire in GR5 is humid climate grass. Load is greater than GR3 but depth is lower, about 1 to 2 feet.

Fine fuel load (t/ac)	2.9
Characteristic SAV (ft⁻1)	1631
Packing ratio (dimensionless)	0.00277
Extinction moisture content (percent)	40

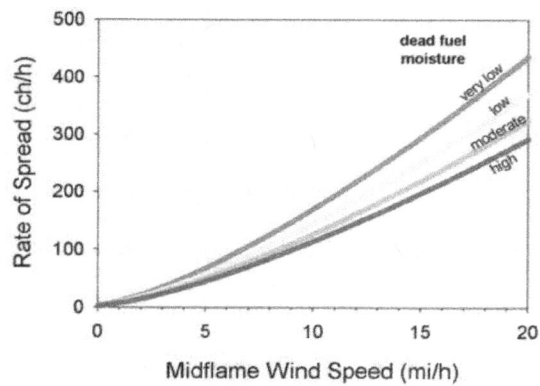 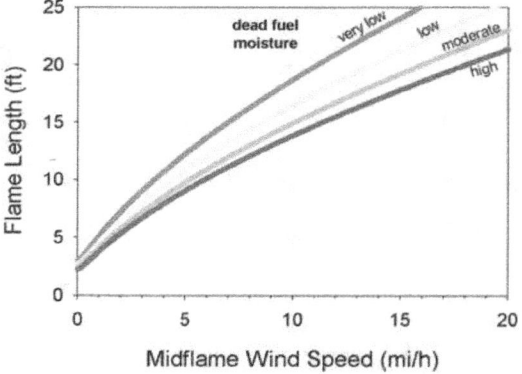

30

USDA Forest Service Gen. Tech. Rep. RMRS-GTR-153. 2005

GR6 (106)

Moderate Load, Humid Climate Grass (Dynamic)

Description: The primary carrier of fire in GR6 is continuous humid climate grass.

Load is greater than GR5 but depth is about the same. Grass is less coarse than GR5.

Fine fuel load (t/ac)	3.5
Characteristic SAV (ft 1)	2006
Packing ratio (dimensionless)	0.00335
Extinction moisture content (percent)	40

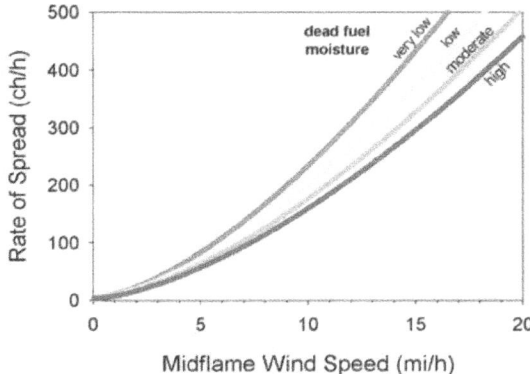 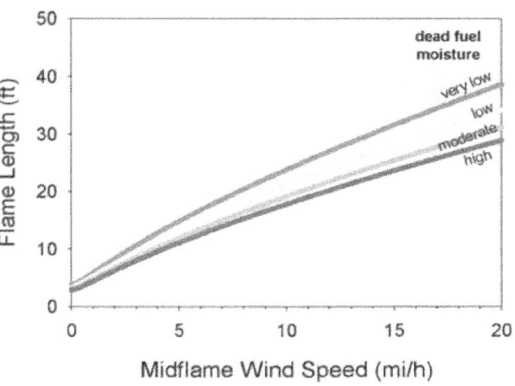

USDA Forest Service Gen. Tech. Rep. RMRS-GTR-153. 2005

31

High Load, Dry Climate Grass (Dynamic)

Description: The primary carrier of fire in GR7 is continuous dry climate grass. Load and depth are greater than GR4. Grass is about 3 feet tall.

Fine fuel load (t/ac)	6.4
Characteristic SAV (ft 1)	1834
Packing ratio (dimensionless)	0.00306
Extinction moisture content (percent)	15

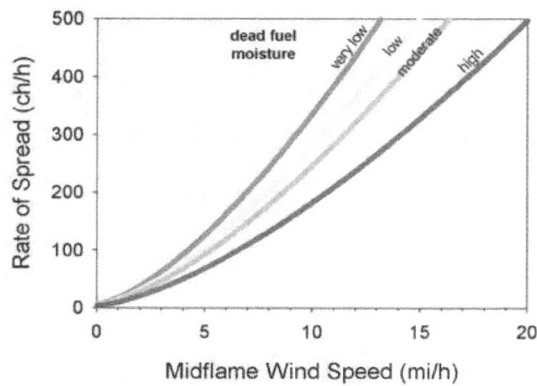
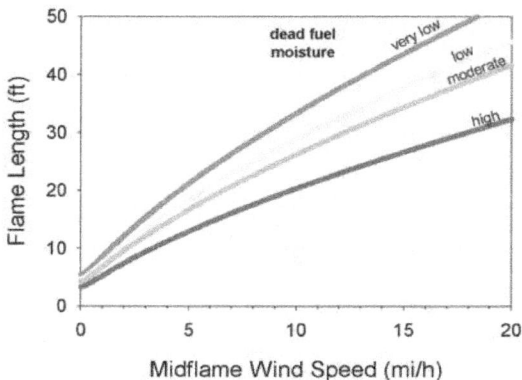

32

USDA Forest Service Gen. Tech. Rep. RMRS-GTR-153. 2005

GR8 (108)

High Load, Very Coarse, Humid Climate Grass (Dynamic)

Description: The primary carrier of fire in GR8 is continuous, very coarse, humid climate grass. Load and depth are greater than GR6. Spread rate and flame length can be extreme if grass is fully cured.

Fine fuel load (t/ac)	7.8
Characteristic SAV (ft 1)	1302
Packing ratio (dimensionless)	0.00316
Extinction moisture content (percent)	30

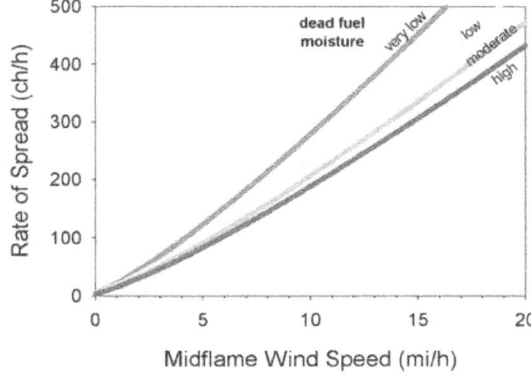 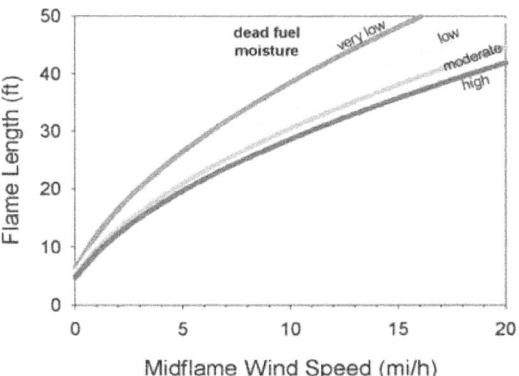

USDA Forest Service Gen. Tech. Rep. RMRS-GTR-153. 2005

33

GR9 (109)

Very High Load, Humid Climate Grass (Dynamic)

Description: The primary carrier of fire in GR9 is dense, tall, humid climate grass. Load and depth are greater than GR8, about 6 feet tall. Spread rate and flame length can be extreme if grass is fully or mostly cured.

Fine fuel load (t/ac)	10.0
Characteristic SAV (ft 1)	1612
Packing ratio (dimensionless)	0.00316
Extinction moisture content (percent)	40

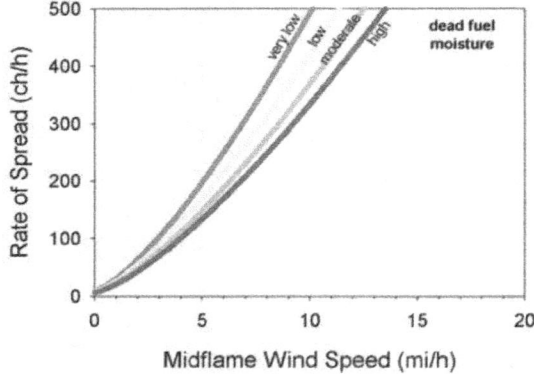 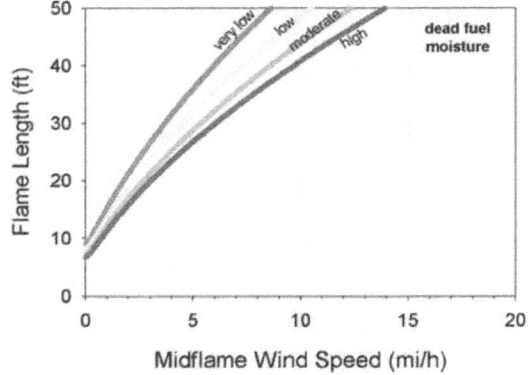

34

USDA Forest Service Gen. Tech. Rep. RMRS-GTR-153. 2005

Grass-Shrub Fuel Type Models (GS)

The primary carrier of fire in the GS fuel models is grass and shrubs combined; both components are important in determining fire behavior.

All GS fuel models are dynamic, meaning that their live herbaceous fuel load shifts from live to dead as a function of live herbaceous moisture content. The effect of live herbaceous moisture content on spread rate and intensity is strong and depends on the relative amount of grass and shrub load in the fuel model.

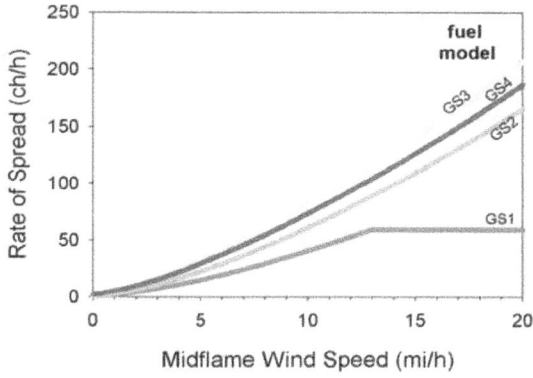
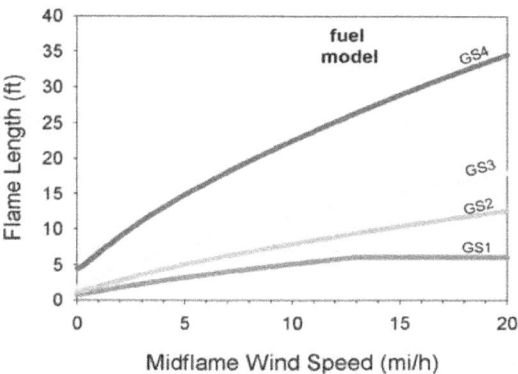

USDA Forest Service Gen. Tech. Rep. RMRS-GTR-153. 2005

35

GS1 (121)

Low Load, Dry Climate Grass-Shrub (Dynamic)

Description: The primary carrier of fire in GS1 is grass and shrubs combined. Shrubs are about 1 foot high, grass load is low. Spread rate is moderate; flame length low. Moisture of extinction is low.

Fine fuel load (t/ac)	1.35
Characteristic SAV (ft 1)	1832
Packing ratio (dimensionless)	0.00215
Extinction moisture content (percent)	15

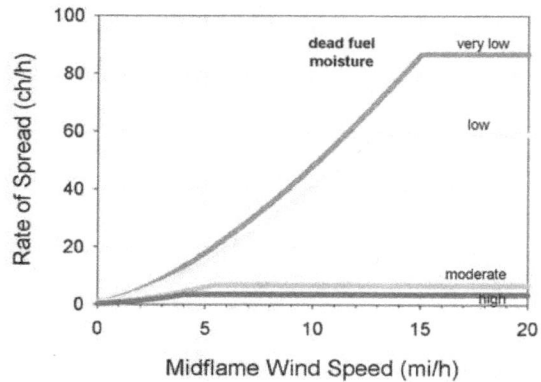 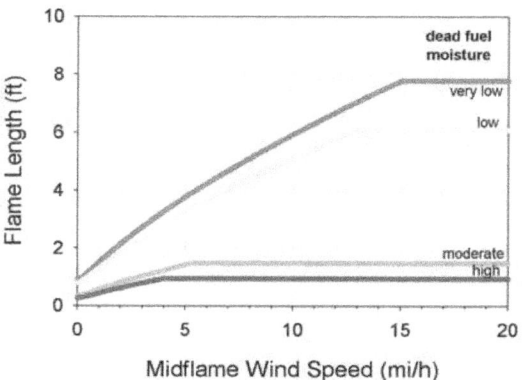

36

USDA Forest Service Gen. Tech. Rep. RMRS-GTR-153. 2005

GS2 (122)

Moderate Load, Dry Climate Grass-Shrub (Dynamic)

Description: The primary carrier of fire in GS2 is grass and shrubs combined. Shrubs are 1 to 3 feet high, grass load is moderate. Spread rate is high; flame length moderate. Moisture of extinction is low.

Fine fuel load (t/ac)	2.1
Characteristic SAV (ft 1)	1827
Packing ratio (dimensionless)	0.00249
Extinction moisture content (percent)	15

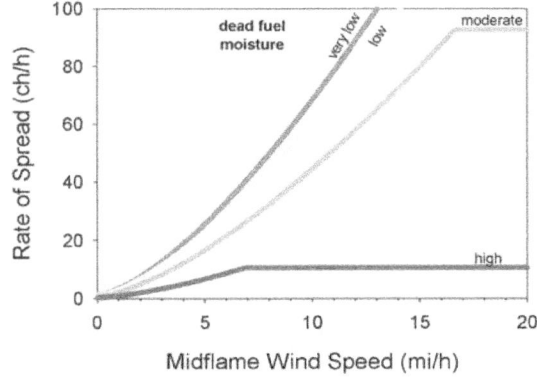 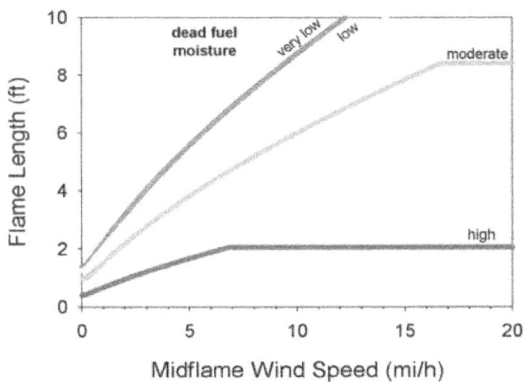

USDA Forest Service Gen. Tech. Rep. RMRS-GTR-153. 2005

37

GS3 (123)

Moderate Load, Humid Climate Grass-Shrub (Dynamic)

Description: The primary carrier of fire in GS3 is grass and shrubs combined. Moderate grass/shrub load, average grass/shrub depth less than 2 feet. Spread rate is high; flame length moderate. Moisture of extinction is high.

Fine fuel load (t/ac)	3.0
Characteristic SAV (ft 1)	1614
Packing ratio (dimensionless)	0.00259
Extinction moisture content (percent)	40

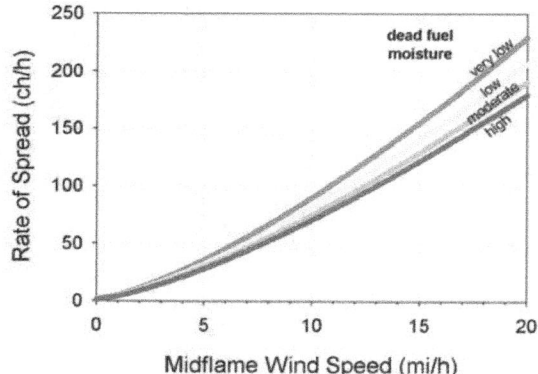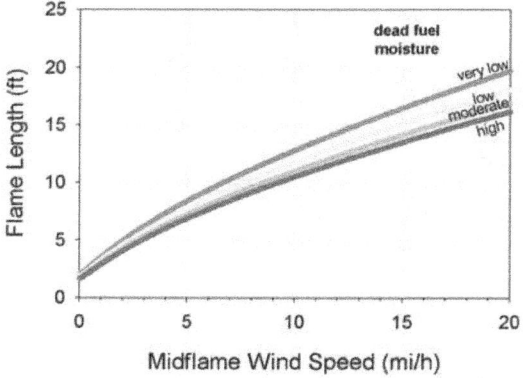

GS4 (124)

High Load, Humid Climate Grass-Shrub (Dynamic)

Description: The primary carrier of fire in GS4 is grass and shrubs combined. Heavy grass/shrub load, depth greater than 2 feet. Spread rate high; flame length very high. Moisture of extinction is high.

Fine fuel load (t/ac)	12.4
Characteristic SAV (ft 1)	1674
Packing ratio (dimensionless)	0.00874
Extinction moisture content (percent)	40

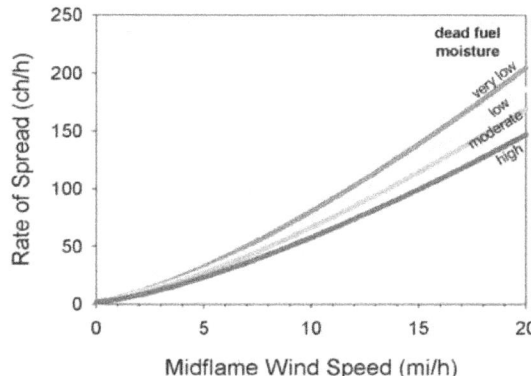
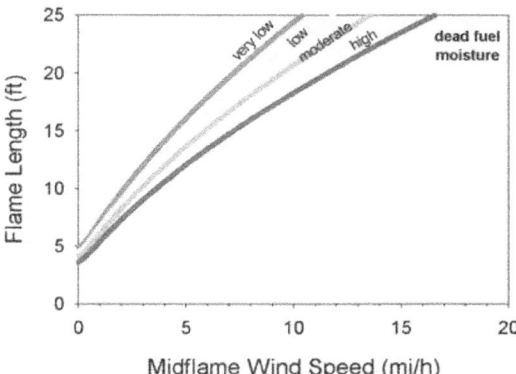

USDA Forest Service Gen. Tech. Rep. RMRS-GTR-153. 2005

39

Shrub Fuel Type Models (SH)

The primary carrier of fire in the SH fuel models is live and dead shrub twigs and foliage in combination with dead and down shrub litter. A small amount of herbaceous fuel may be present, especially in SH1 and SH9, which are dynamic models (their live herbaceous fuel load shifts from live to dead as a function of live herbaceous moisture content). The effect of live herbaceous moisture content on spread rate and flame length can be strong in those dynamic SH models.

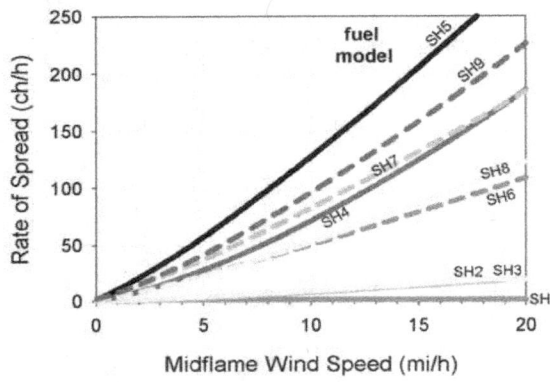

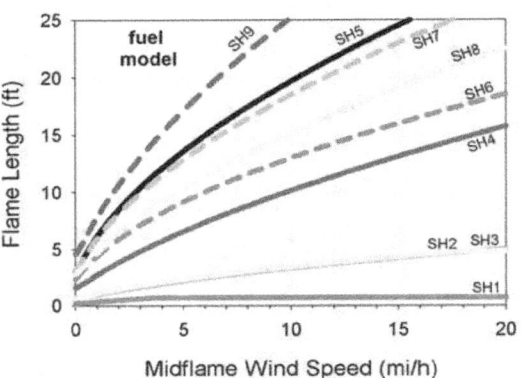

40

USDA Forest Service Gen. Tech. Rep. RMRS-GTR-153. 2005

SH1 (141)

Low Load Dry Climate Shrub (Dynamic)

Description: The primary carrier of fire in SH1 is woody shrubs and shrub litter. Low shrub fuel load, fuelbed depth about 1 foot; some grass may be present. Spread rate is very low; flame length very low.

Fine fuel load (t/ac)	1.7
Characteristic SAV (ft 1)	1674
Packing ratio (dimensionless)	0.00280
Extinction moisture content (percent)	15

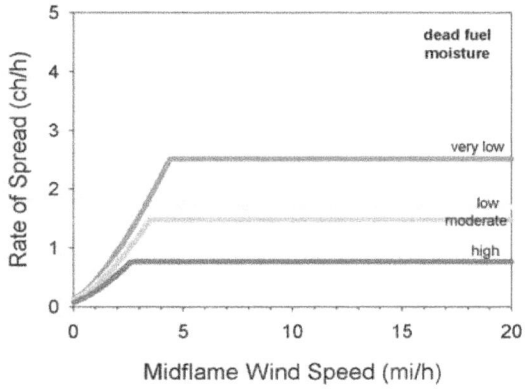 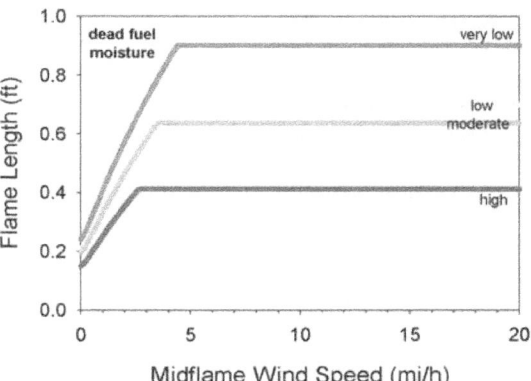

USDA Forest Service Gen. Tech. Rep. RMRS-GTR-153. 2005

41

SH2 (142)

Moderate Load Dry Climate Shrub

Description: The primary carrier of fire in SH2 is woody shrubs and shrub litter.

Moderate fuel load (higher than SH1), depth about 1 foot, no grass fuel present.

Spread rate is low; flame length low.

Fine fuel load (t/ac)	5.2
Characteristic SAV (ft 1)	1672
Packing ratio (dimensionless)	0.01198
Extinction moisture content (percent)	15

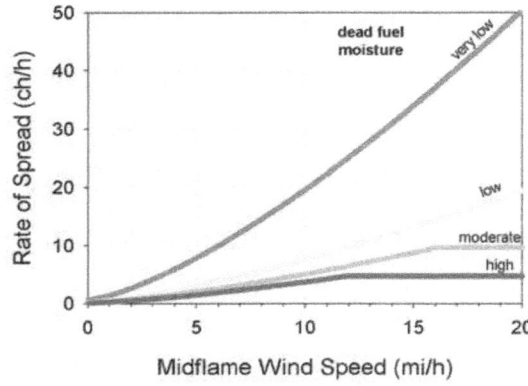 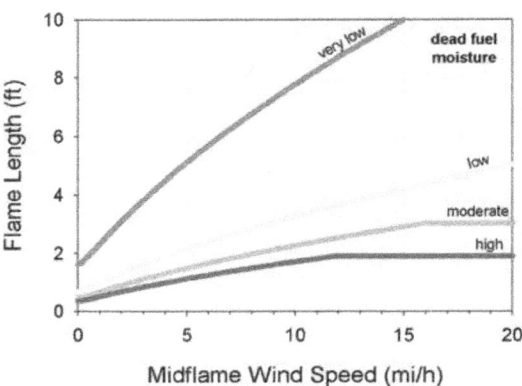

SH3 (143)

Moderate Load, Humid Climate Shrub

Description: The primary carrier of fire in SH3 is woody shrubs and shrub litter.

Moderate shrub load, possibly with pine overstory or herbaceous fuel, fuel bed depth

2 to 3 feet. Spread rate is low; flame length low.

Fine fuel load (t/ac)	6.65
Characteristic SAV (ft 1)	1371
Packing ratio (dimensionless)	0.00577
Extinction moisture content (percent)	40

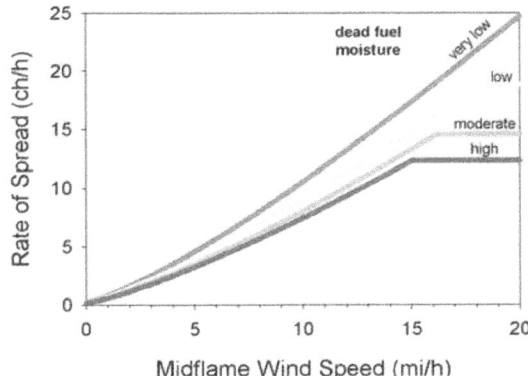 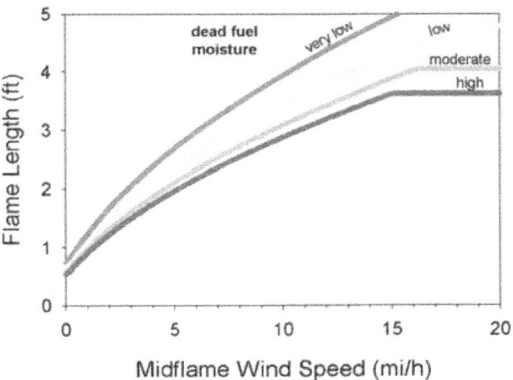

USDA Forest Service Gen. Tech. Rep. RMRS-GTR-153. 2005

43

SH4 (144)

Low Load, Humid Climate Timber-Shrub

Description: The primary carrier of fire in SH4 is woody shrubs and shrub litter. Low to moderate shrub and litter load, possibly with pine overstory, fuel bed depth about 3 feet. Spread rate is high; flame length moderate.

Fine fuel load (t/ac)	3.4
Characteristic SAV (ft 1)	1682
Packing ratio (dimensionless)	0.00227
Extinction moisture content (percent)	30

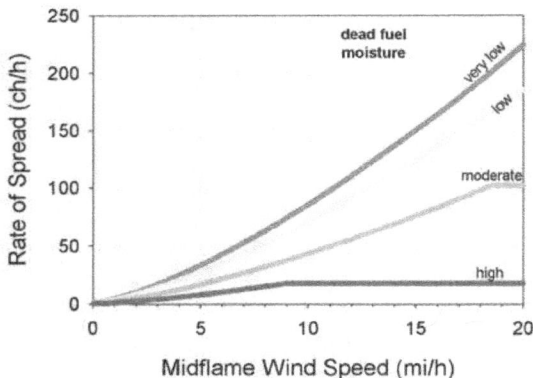 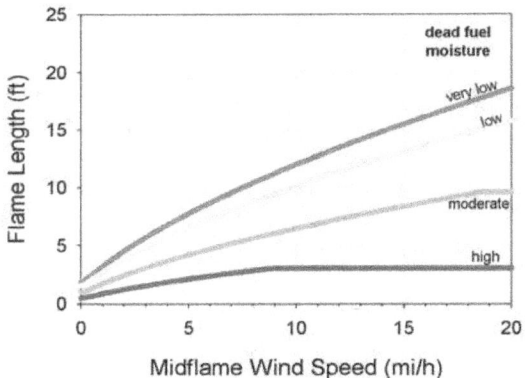

44

USDA Forest Service Gen. Tech. Rep. RMRS-GTR-153. 2005

SH5 (145)

High Load, Dry Climate Shrub

Description: The primary carrier of fire in SH5 is woody shrubs and shrub litter. Heavy shrub load, depth 4 6 feet. Spread rate very high; flame length very high. Moisture of extinction is high.

Fine fuel load (t/ac)	6.5
Characteristic SAV (ft 1)	1252
Packing ratio (dimensionless)	0.00206
Extinction moisture content (percent)	15

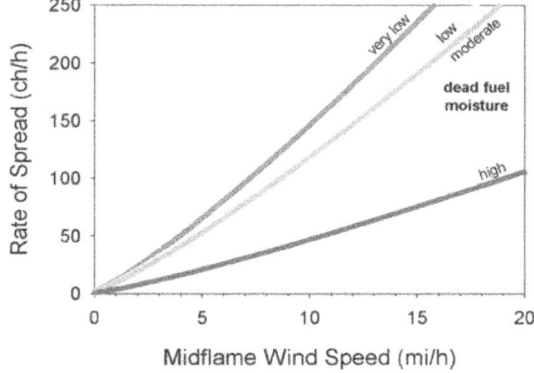 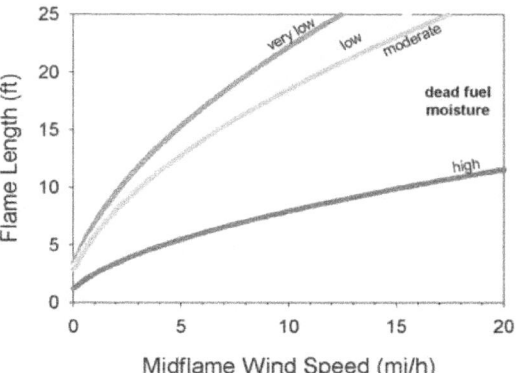

USDA Forest Service Gen. Tech. Rep. RMRS-GTR-153. 2005

45

SH6 (146)

Low Load, Humid Climate Shrub

Description: The primary carrier of fire in SH6 is woody shrubs and shrub litter. Dense shrubs, little or no herbaceous fuel, fuelbed depth about 2 feet. Spread rate is high; flame length high.

Fine fuel load (t/ac)	4.3
Characteristic SAV (ft 1)	1144
Packing ratio (dimensionless)	0.00412
Extinction moisture content (percent)	30

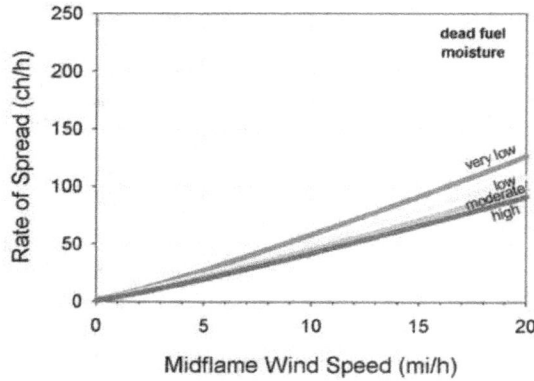 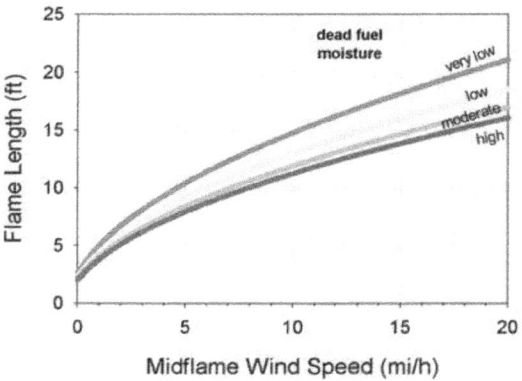

46

USDA Forest Service Gen. Tech. Rep. RMRS-GTR-153. 2005

SH7 (147)

Very High Load, Dry Climate Shrub

Description: The primary carrier of fire in SH7 is woody shrubs and shrub litter. Very heavy shrub load, depth 4 to 6 feet. Spread rate lower than SH7, but flame length similar. Spread rate is high; flame length very high.

Fine fuel load (t/ac)	6.9
Characteristic SAV (ft 1)	1233
Packing ratio (dimensionless)	0.00344
Extinction moisture content (percent)	15

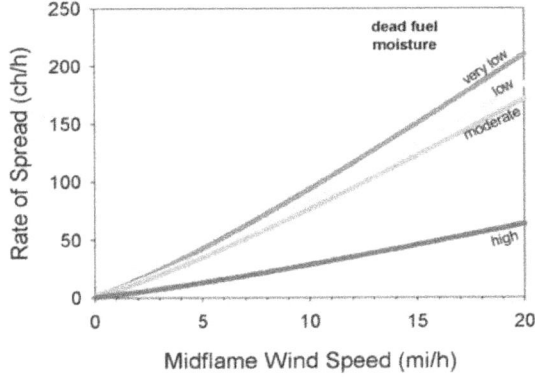 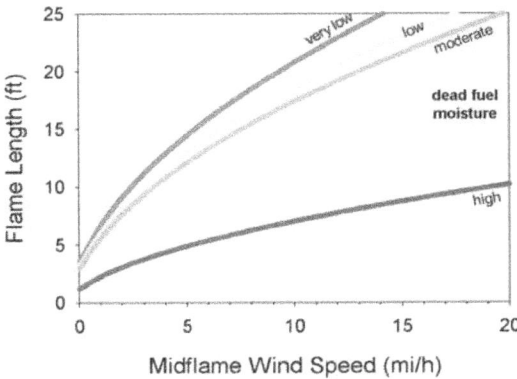

USDA Forest Service Gen. Tech. Rep. RMRS-GTR-153. 2005

47

SH8 (148)

High Load, Humid Climate Shrub

Description: The primary carrier of fire in SH8 is woody shrubs and shrub litter. Dense shrubs, little or no herbaceous fuel, fuelbed depth about 3 feet. Spread rate is high; flame length high.

Fine fuel load (t/ac)	6.4
Characteristic SAV (ft 1)	1386
Packing ratio (dimensionless)	0.00509
Extinction moisture content (percent)	40

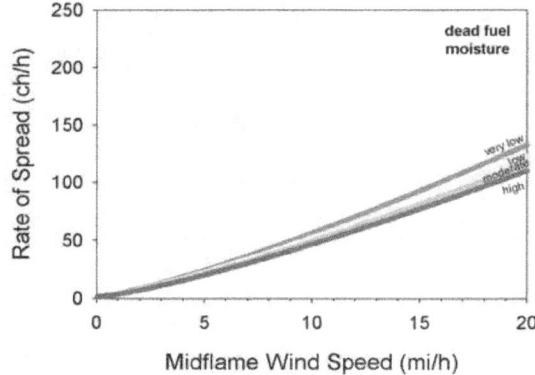
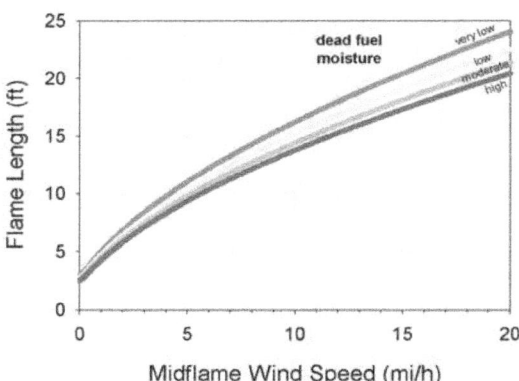

SH9 (149)

Very High Load, Humid Climate Shrub (Dynamic)

Description: The primary carrier of fire in SH9 is woody shrubs and shrub litter.

Dense, finely branched shrubs with significant fine dead fuel, about 4 to 6 feet tall;

some herbaceous fuel may be present. Spread rate is high, flame length very high.

Fine fuel load (t/ac)	13.05
Characteristic SAV (ft 1)	1378
Packing ratio (dimensionless)	0.00505
Extinction moisture content (percent)	40

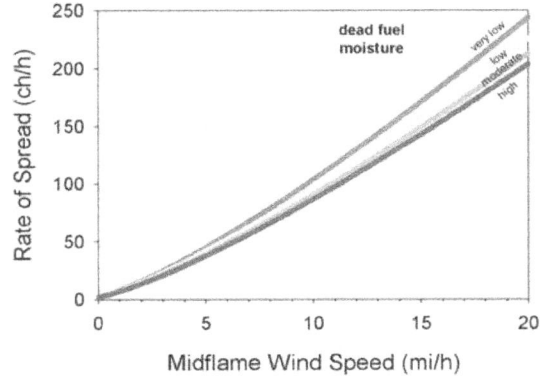 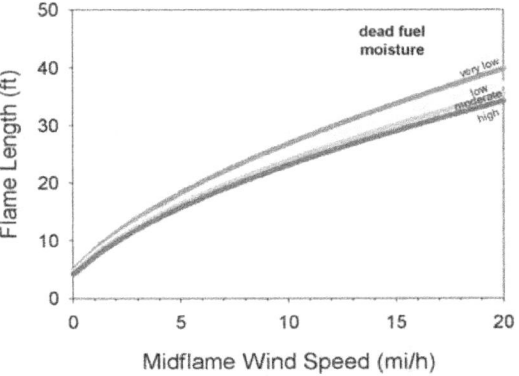

USDA Forest Service Gen. Tech. Rep. RMRS-GTR-153. 2005

49

Timber-Understory Fuel Type Models (TU)

The primary carrier of fire in the TU fuel models is forest litter in combination with herbaceous or shrub fuels. TU1 and TU3 contain live herbaceous load and are dynamic, meaning that their live herbaceous fuel load is allocated between live and dead as a function of live herbaceous moisture content. The effect of live herbaceous moisture content on spread rate and intensity is strong and depends on the relative amount of grass and shrub load in the fuel model.

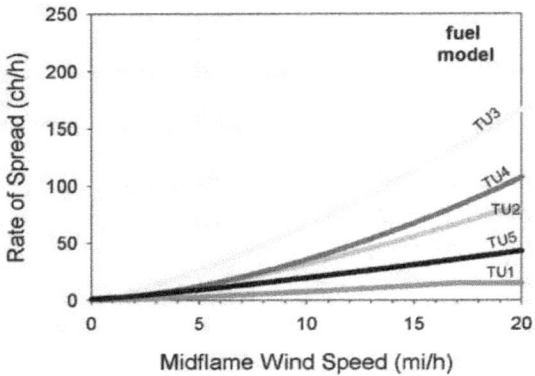
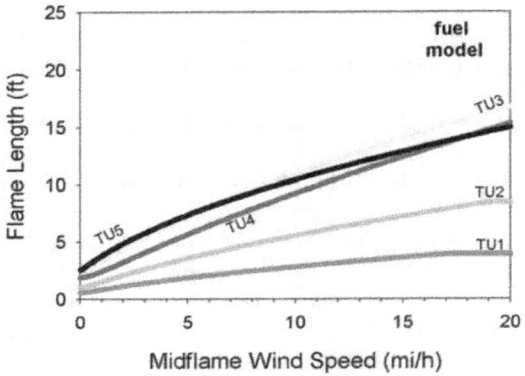

50

USDA Forest Service Gen. Tech. Rep. RMRS-GTR-153. 2005

TU1 (161)

Low Load Dry Climate Timber-Grass-Shrub (Dynamic)

Description: The primary carrier of fire in TU1 is low load of grass and/or shrub with litter. Spread rate is low; flame length low.

Fine fuel load (t/ac)	1.3
Characteristic SAV (ft 1)	1606
Packing ratio (dimensionless)	0.00885
Extinction moisture content (percent)	20

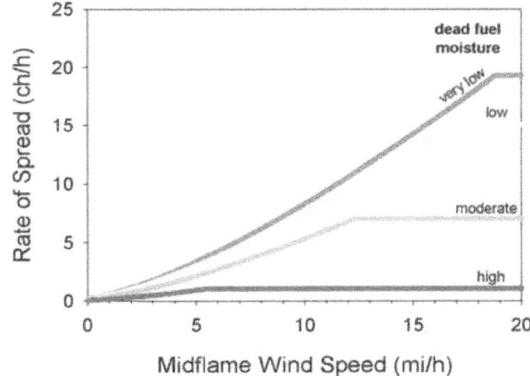 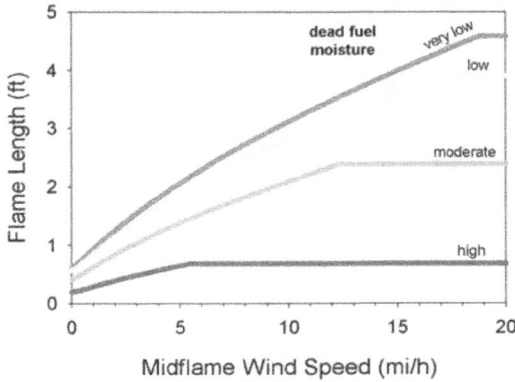

USDA Forest Service Gen. Tech. Rep. RMRS-GTR-153. 2005

51

TU2 (162)

Moderate Load, Humid Climate Timber-Shrub

Description: The primary carrier of fire in TU2 is moderate litter load with shrub component. High extinction moisture. Spread rate is moderate; flame length low.

Fine fuel load (t/ac)	1.15
Characteristic SAV (ft 1)	1767
Packing ratio (dimensionless)	0.00603
Extinction moisture content (percent)	30

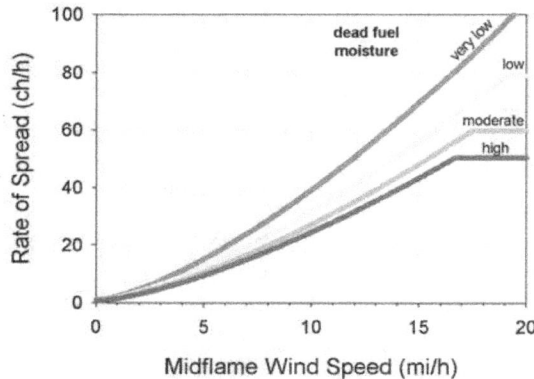 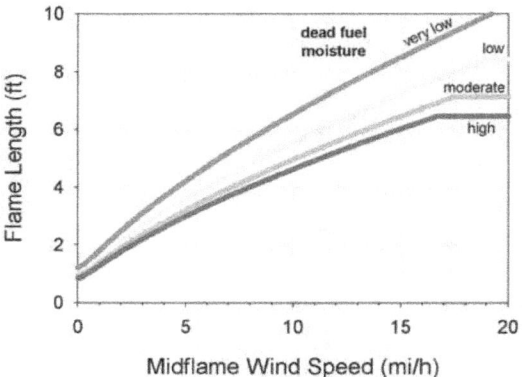

52

USDA Forest Service Gen. Tech. Rep. RMRS-GTR-153. 2005

TU3 (163)

Moderate Load, Humid Climate Timber-Grass-Shrub (Dynamic)

Description: The primary carrier of fire in TU3 is moderate forest litter with grass and shrub components. Extinction moisture is high. Spread rate is high; flame length moderate.

Fine fuel load (t/ac)	2.85
Characteristic SAV (ft 1)	1611
Packing ratio (dimensionless)	0.00359
Extinction moisture content (percent)	30

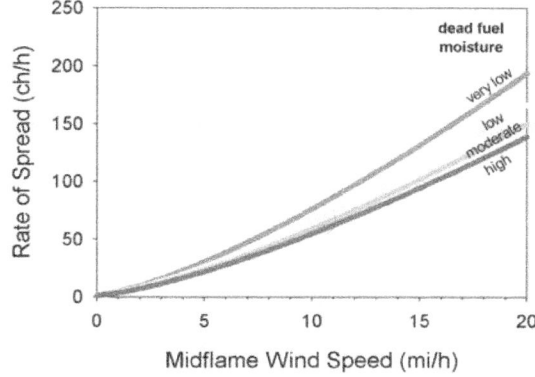 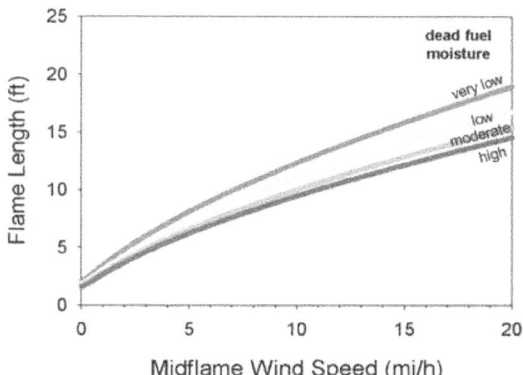

USDA Forest Service Gen. Tech. Rep. RMRS-GTR-153. 2005

53

TU4 (164)

Dwarf Conifer With Understory

Description: The primary carrier of fire in TU4 is short conifer trees with grass or moss understory. Spread rate is moderate; flame length moderate.

Fine fuel load (t/ac)	6.5
Characteristic SAV (ft 1)	2216
Packing ratio (dimensionless)	0.01865
Extinction moisture content (percent)	12

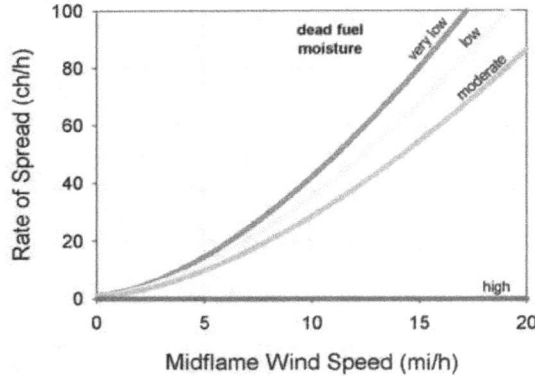 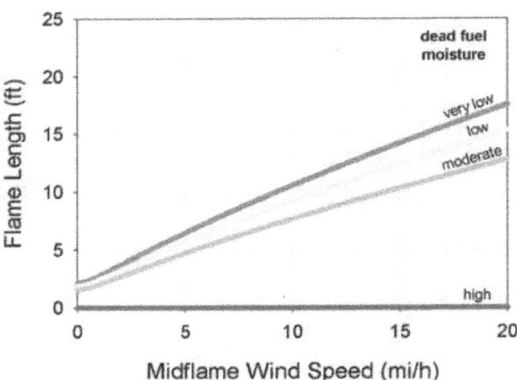

54

USDA Forest Service Gen. Tech. Rep. RMRS-GTR-153. 2005

TU5 (165)

Very High Load, Dry Climate Timber-Shrub

Description: The primary carrier of fire in TU5 is heavy forest litter with a shrub or small tree understory. Spread rate is moderate; flame length moderate.

Fine fuel load (t/ac)	7.0
Characteristic SAV (ft 1)	1224
Packing ratio (dimensionless)	0.02009
Extinction moisture content (percent)	25

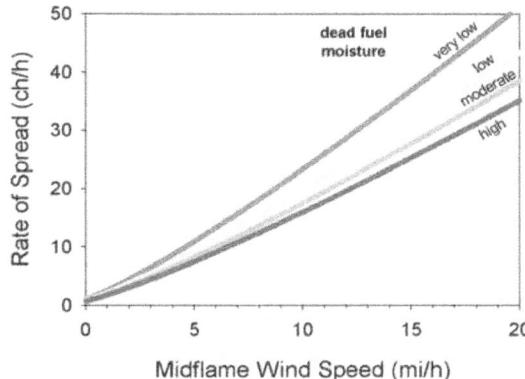 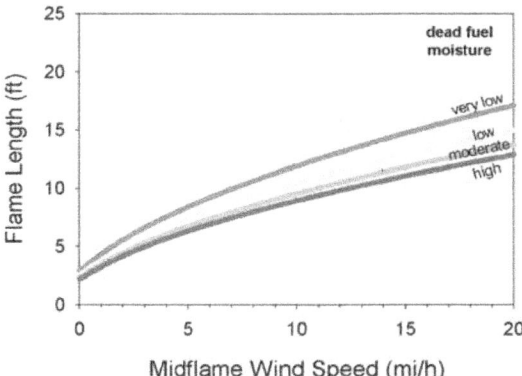

USDA Forest Service Gen. Tech. Rep. RMRS-GTR-153. 2005

55

Timber Litter Fuel Type Models (TL)

The primary carrier of fire in the TL fuel models is dead and down woody fuel. Live fuel, if present, has little effect on fire behavior.

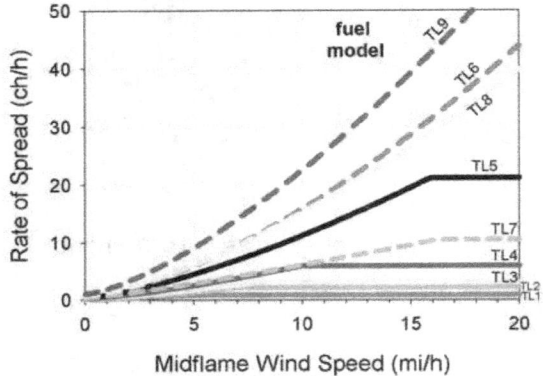
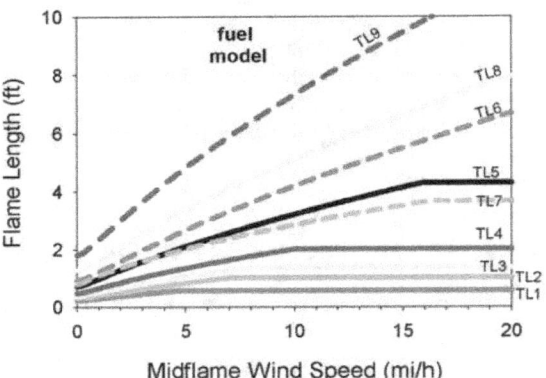

56

USDA Forest Service Gen. Tech. Rep. RMRS-GTR-153. 2005

TL1 (181)

Low Load Compact Conifer Litter

Description: The primary carrier of fire in TL1 is compact forest litter. Light to moderate load, fuels 1 to 2 inches deep. May be used to represent a recently burned forest. Spread rate is very low; flame length very low.

Fine fuel load (t/ac)	1.0
Characteristic SAV (ft 1)	1716
Packing ratio (dimensionless)	0.04878
Extinction moisture content (percent)	30

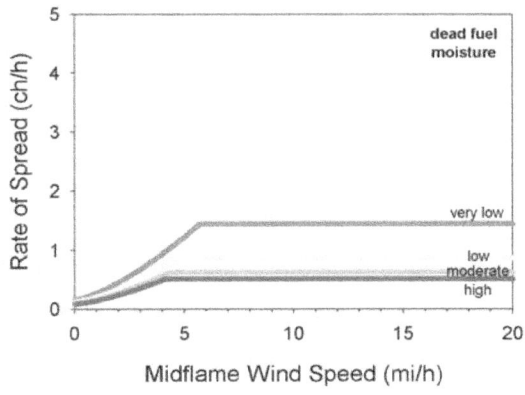 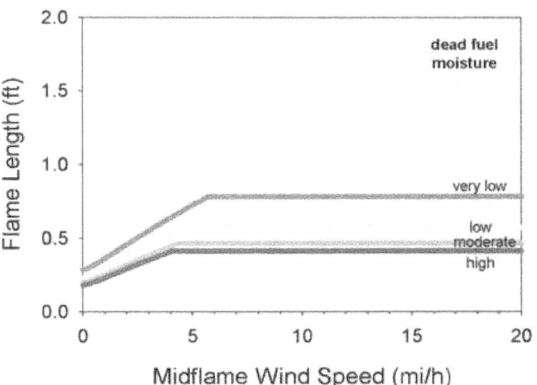

USDA Forest Service Gen. Tech. Rep. RMRS-GTR-153. 2005

57

TL2 (182)

Low Load Broadleaf Litter

Description: The primary carrier of fire in TL2 is broadleaf (hardwood) litter. Low load, compact broadleaf litter. Spread rate is very low; flame length very low.

Fine fuel load (t/ac)	1.4
Characteristic SAV (ft 1)	1806
Packing ratio (dimensionless)	0.04232
Extinction moisture content (percent)	25

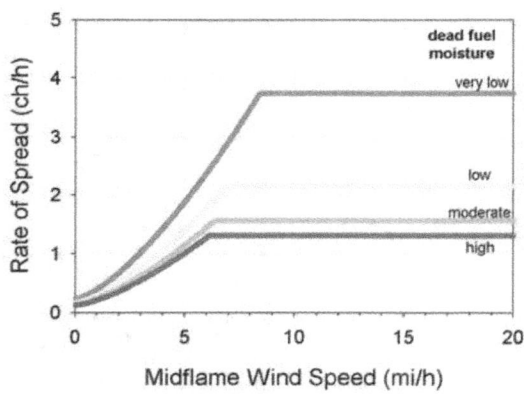 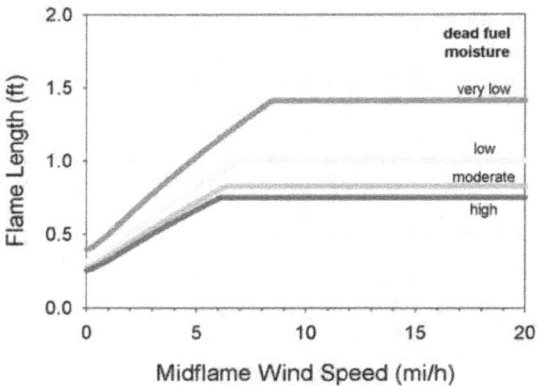

TL3 (183)

Moderate Load Conifer Litter

Description: The primary carrier of fire in TL3 is moderate load conifer litter, light load of coarse fuels. Spread rate is very low; flame length low.

Fine fuel load (t/ac)	0.50
Characteristic SAV (ft 1)	1532
Packing ratio (dimensionless)	0.02630
Extinction moisture content (percent)	20

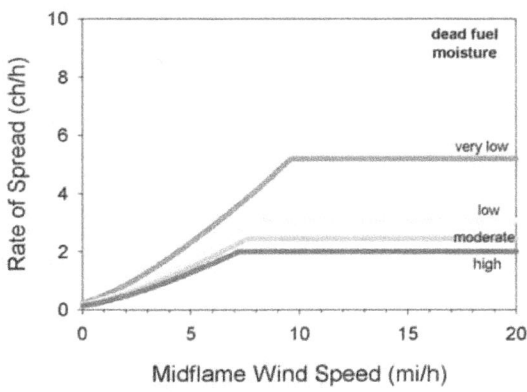 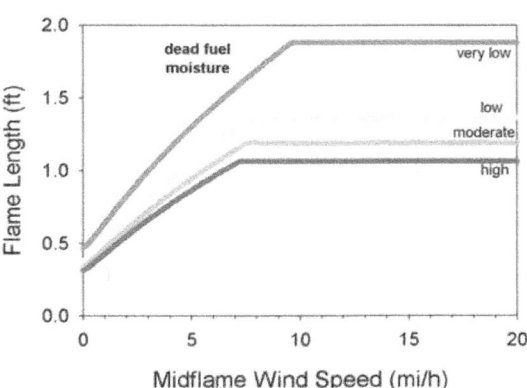

USDA Forest Service Gen. Tech. Rep. RMRS-GTR-153. 2005

59

TL4 (184)

Small downed logs

Description: The primary carrier of fire in TL4 is moderate load of fine litter and coarse fuels. Includes small diameter downed logs. Spread rate is low; flame length low.

Fine fuel load (t/ac)	0.50
Characteristic SAV (ft 1)	1568
Packing ratio (dimensionless)	0.02224
Extinction moisture content (percent)	25

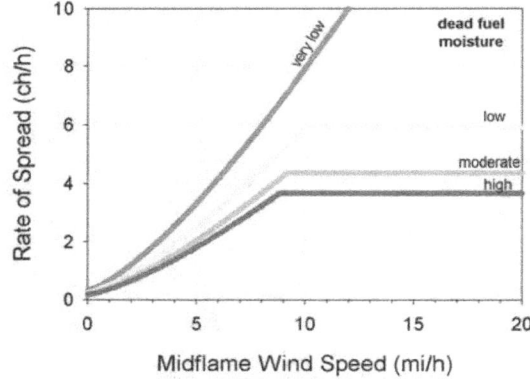 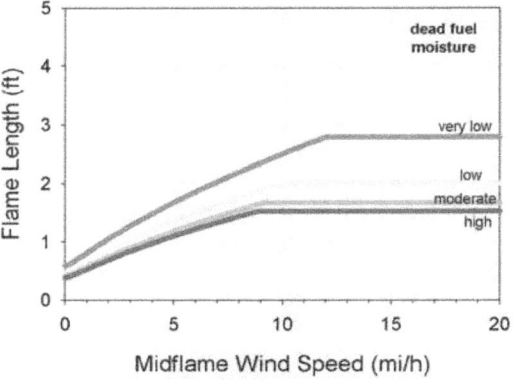

TL5 (185)

High Load Conifer Litter

Description: The primary carrier of fire in TL5 is high load conifer litter; light slash or mortality fuel. Spread rate is low; flame length low.

Fine fuel load (t/ac)	1.15
Characteristic SAV (ft 1)	1713
Packing ratio (dimensionless)	0.01925
Extinction moisture content (percent)	25

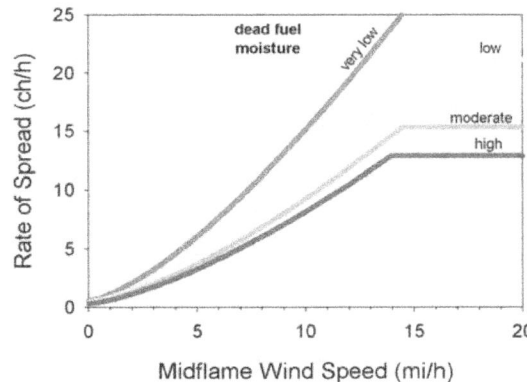 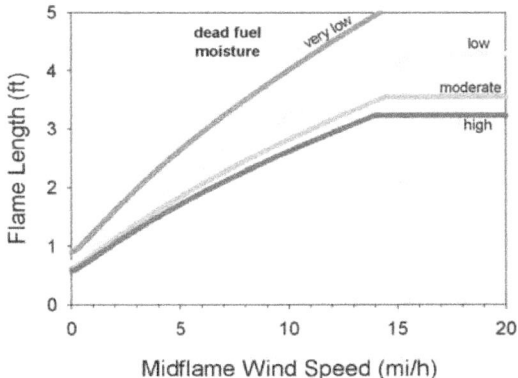

USDA Forest Service Gen. Tech. Rep. RMRS-GTR-153. 2005

61

TL6 (186)

Moderate Load Broadleaf Litter

Description: The primary carrier of fire in TL6 is moderate load broadleaf litter, less compact than TL2. Spread rate is moderate; flame length low.

Fine fuel load (t/ac)	2.4
Characteristic SAV (ft 1)	1936
Packing ratio (dimensionless)	0.02296
Extinction moisture content (percent)	25

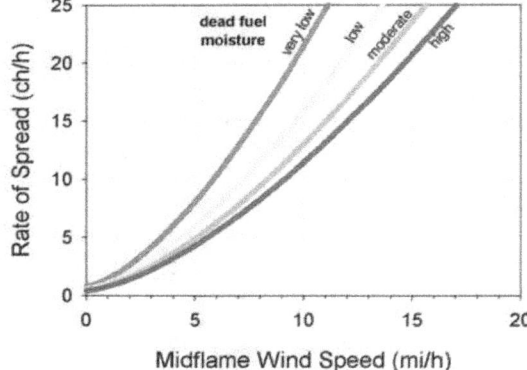 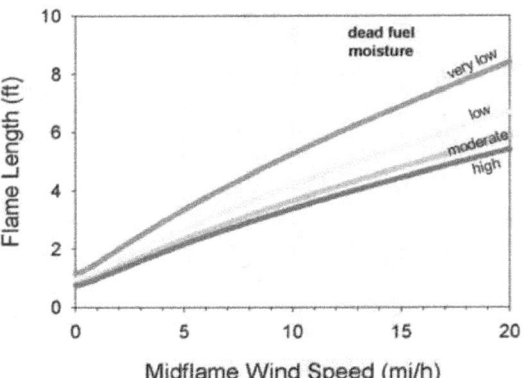

TL7 (187)

Large Downed Logs

Description: The primary carrier of fire in TL7 is heavy load forest litter, includes larger diameter downed logs. Spread rate low; flame length low.

Fine fuel load (t/ac)	0.30
Characteristic SAV (ft 1)	1229
Packing ratio (dimensionless)	0.03515
Extinction moisture content (percent)	25

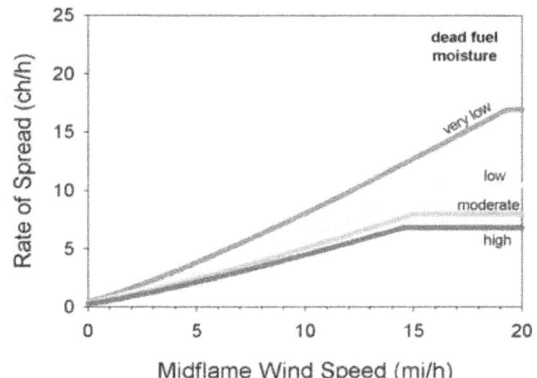 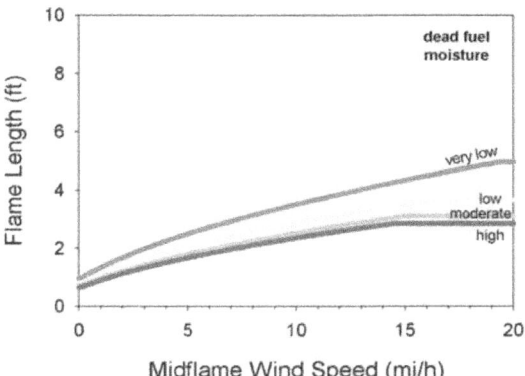

USDA Forest Service Gen. Tech. Rep. RMRS-GTR-153. 2005

63

TL8 (188)

Long-Needle Litter

Description: The primary carrier of fire in TL8 is moderate load long needle pine litter, may include small amount of herbaceous load. Spread rate is moderate; flame length low.

Fine fuel load (t/ac)	5.8
Characteristic SAV (ft 1)	1770
Packing ratio (dimensionless)	0.03969
Extinction moisture content (percent)	35

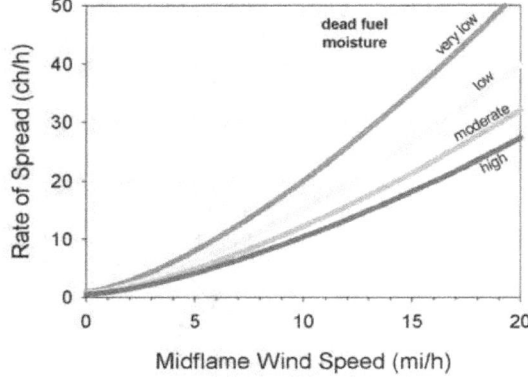 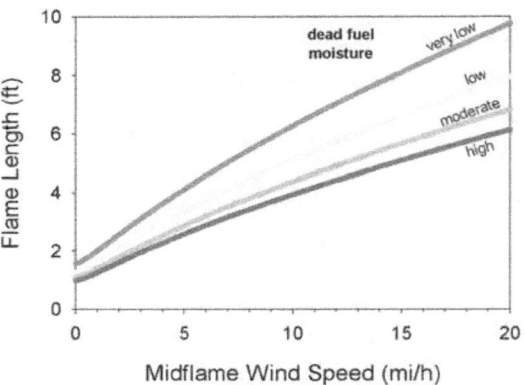

64

USDA Forest Service Gen. Tech. Rep. RMRS-GTR-153. 2005

TL9 (189)

Very High Load Broadleaf Litter

Description: The primary carrier of fire in TL9 is very high load, fluffy broadleaf litter. TL9 can also be used to represent heavy needle drape. Spread rate is moderate; flame length moderate.

Fine fuel load (t/ac)	6.65
Characteristic SAV (ft 1)	1733
Packing ratio (dimensionless)	0.03372
Extinction moisture content (percent)	35

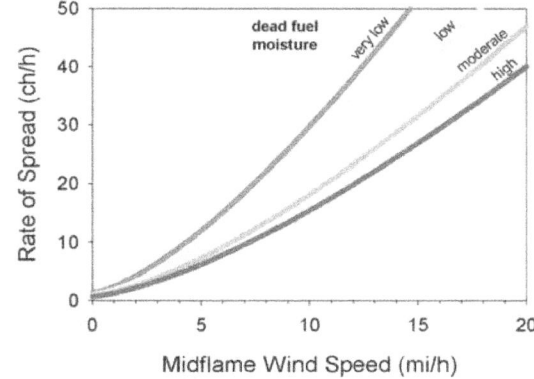

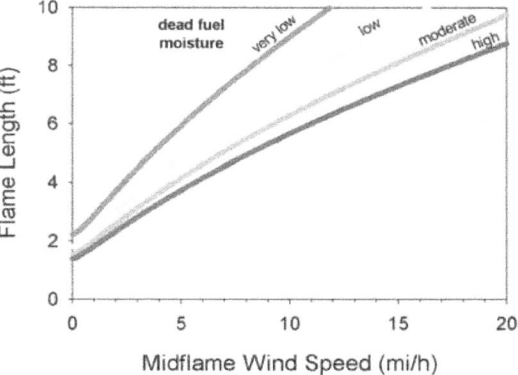

USDA Forest Service Gen. Tech. Rep. RMRS-GTR-153. 2005

65

Slash-Blowdown Fuel Type Models (SB)

The primary carrier of fire in the SB fuel models is activity fuel or blowdown.
Forested areas with heavy mortality may be modeled with SB fuel models.

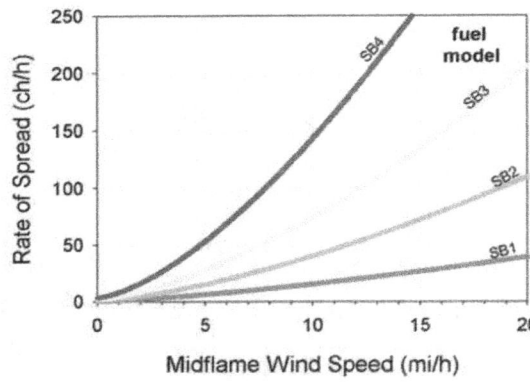 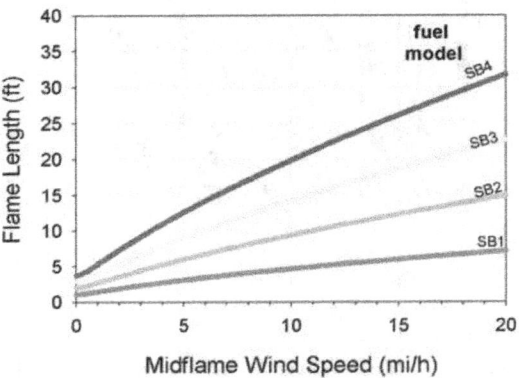

USDA Forest Service Gen. Tech. Rep. RMRS-GTR-153. 2005

SB1 (201)

Low Load Activity Fuel

Description: The primary carrier of fire in SB1 is light dead and down activity fuel. Fine fuel load is 10 to 20 t/ac, weighted toward fuels 1 to 3 inches diameter class, depth is less than 1 foot. Spread rate is moderate; flame length low.

Fine fuel load (t/ac)	1.50
Characteristic SAV (ft 1)	1653
Packing ratio (dimensionless)	0.02224
Extinction moisture content (percent)	25

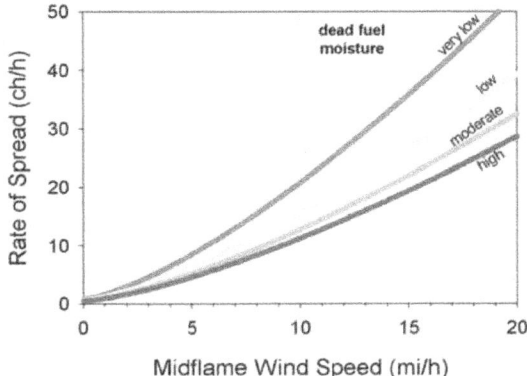 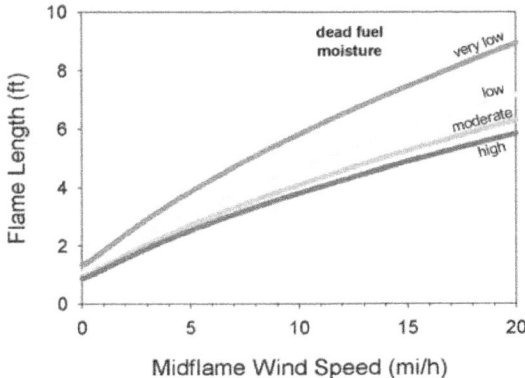

USDA Forest Service Gen. Tech. Rep. RMRS-GTR-153. 2005

67

SB2 (202)

Moderate Load Activity Fuel or Low Load Blowdown

Description: The primary carrier of fire in SB2 is moderate dead and down activity fuel or light blowdown. Fine fuel load is 7 to 12 t/ac, evenly distributed across 0 to 0.25, 0.25 to 1, and 1 to 3 inch diameter classes, depth is about 1 foot. Blowdown is scattered, with many trees still standing. Spread rate is moderate; flame length moderate.

Fine fuel load (t/ac)	4.5
Characteristic SAV (ft 1)	1884
Packing ratio (dimensionless)	0.01829
Extinction moisture content (percent)	25

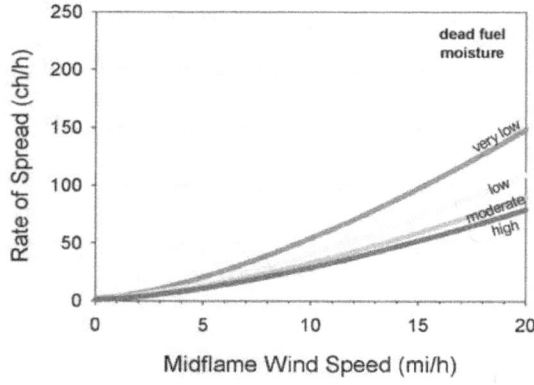 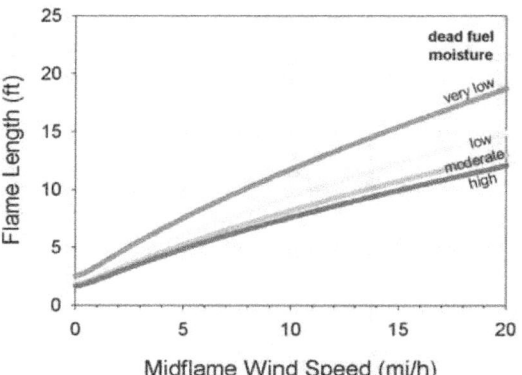

68

USDA Forest Service Gen. Tech. Rep. RMRS-GTR-153. 2005

SB3 (203)

High Load Activity Fuel or Moderate Load Blowdown

Description: The primary carrier of fire in SB3 is heavy dead and down activity fuel or moderate blowdown. Fine fuel load is 7 to 12 t/ac, weighted toward 0 to 0.25 inch diameter class, depth is more than 1 foot. Blowdown is moderate, trees compacted to near the ground. Spread rate is high; flame length high.

Fine fuel load (t/ac)	5.50
Characteristic SAV (ft 1)	1935
Packing ratio (dimensionless)	0.01345
Extinction moisture content (percent)	25

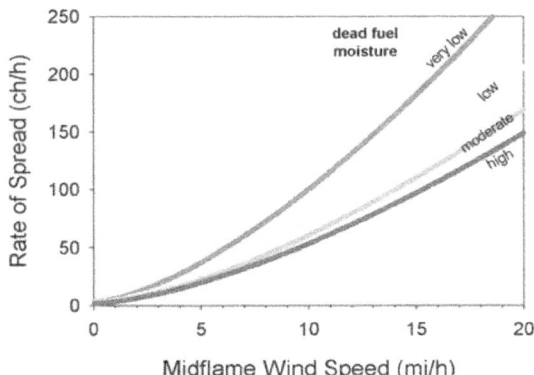 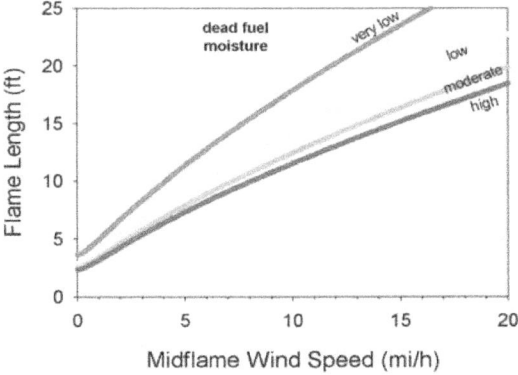

USDA Forest Service Gen. Tech. Rep. RMRS-GTR-153. 2005

69

SB4 (204)

High Load Blowdown

Description: The primary carrier of fire in SB4 is heavy blowdown fuel. Blowdown is total, fuelbed not compacted, most foliage and fine fuel still attached to blowdown. Spread rate very high; flame length very high.

Fine fuel load (t/ac)	5.25
Characteristic SAV (ft 1)	1907
Packing ratio (dimensionless)	0.00744
Extinction moisture content (percent)	25

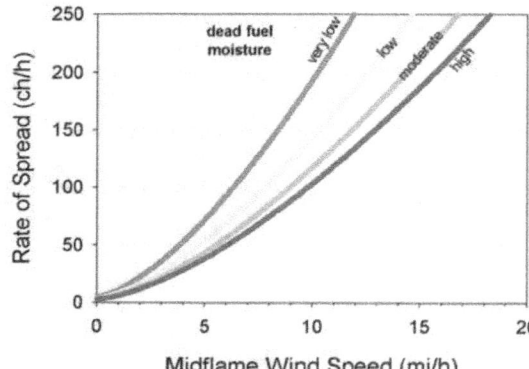 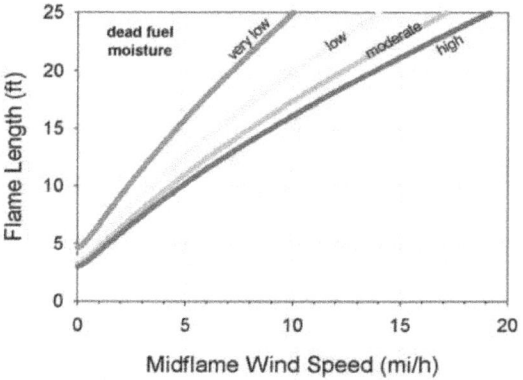

70

USDA Forest Service Gen. Tech. Rep. RMRS-GTR-153. 2005

References

Albini, F. A. 1976. Estimating wildfire behavior and effects. Gen. Tech. Rep. INT-30. Ogden, Utah: Department of Agriculture, Forest Service, Intermountain Forest and Range Experiment Station. 92 p.

Albini, F. A.; Baughman, R. G. 1979. Estimating windspeeds for predicting wildland fire behavior. Res. Pap. INT-221. Ogden, Utah: U.S. Department of Agriculture, Forest Service, Intermountain Forest and Range Experiment Station. 12 p.

Alexander, M. E. 1988. Help with making crown fire hazard assessments. In: Fischer, W. C.; Arno, S. F., comps. Protecting people and homes from wildfire in the Interior West: proceedings of the Symposium and Workshop; 1988 October 6-8; Missoula, MT. Proc. Gen. Tech. Rep. INT-251. Ogden, UT: U.S. Department of Agriculture, Forest Service, Intermountain Research Station: 147-156.

Anderson, H. E. 1982. Aids to determining fuel models for estimating fire behavior. Gen. Tech. Rep. INT-122. Ogden, UT: U.S. Department of Agriculture, Forest Service, Intermountain Forest and Range Experiment Station. 22 p.

Andrews, P. L. 1986. BEHAVE: Fire behavior prediction and fuel modeling system — BURN Subsystem, Part 1. Gen. Tech. Rep. INT-194. Ogden, UT: U.S. Department of Agriculture, Forest Service, Intermountain Forest and Range Experiment Station. 130 p.

Andrews, P. L.; Bevins, C. D.; Seli, R. C. 2003. BehavePlus fire modeling system, version 2.0: User's Guide. Gen. Tech. Rep. RMRS-GTR-106WWW. Ogden, UT: Department of Agriculture, Forest Service, Rocky Mountain Research Station. 132 p.

Andrews, P. L.; Queen, L. P. 2001. Fire modeling and information system technology. Int. J. Wildland Fire 10: 343-352.

Burgan, R. E. 1979. Estimating live fuel moisture for the 1978 National Fire-Danger Rating System. Gen. Tech. Rep. INT-226. Ogden, UT: U.S. Department of Agriculture, Forest Service, Intermountain Forest and Range Experiment Station. 17 p.

Burgan, R. E.; Rothermel, R. C. 1984. BEHAVE: Fire behavior prediction and fuel modeling system – FUEL subsystem. Gen. Tech. Rep. INT-167. Ogden, UT: U.S. Department of Agriculture, Forest Service, Intermountain Forest and Range Experiment Station. 126 p.

Deeming, J. E.; Burgan, R. E.; Cohen, J. D. 1977. The National Fire Danger Rating System. Gen. Tech. Rep. INT-39. Ogden, UT: U.S. Department of Agriculture, Forest Service, Intermountain Forest and Range Experiment Station. 63 p.

Finney, M. A. 1998. FARSITE: Fire Area Simulator—model development and evaluation. Res. Pap. RMRS-RP-4. Fort Collins, CO: U.S. Department of Agriculture, Forest Service, Rocky Mountain Research Station. 47 p.

Ottmar, R. D.; Vihnanek, R. E. 1998. Stereo photo series for quantifying natural fuels. Volume II: black spruce and white spruce types in Alaska. PMS 831. Boise, ID: National Wildfire Coordinating Group, National Interagency Fire Center. 65 p.

Ottmar, R. D.; Vihnanek, R. E. 1999. Stereo photo series for quantifying natural fuels. Volume V: Midwest red and white pine, Northern tallgrass prairie, and mixed oak types in the Central and Lake States. PMS 834. Boise, ID: National Wildfire Coordinating Group, National Interagency Fire Center. 99 p.

Ottmar, R. D.; Vihnanek, R. E. 2000. Stereo photo series for quantifying natural fuels. Volume VI: longleaf pine, pocosin, and marshgrass types in the Southeast United States. PMS 835. Boise, ID: National Wildfire Coordinating Group, National Interagency Fire Center. 56 p.

Ottmar, R. D.; Vihnanek, R. E. 2002. Stereo photo series for quantifying natural fuels. Volume IIa: hardwoods with spruce in Alaska. PMS 836. Boise, ID: National Wildfire Coordinating Group, National Interagency Fire Center. 41 p.

Ottmar, R. D.; Vihnanek, R. E.; Mathey, J. W. 2003. Stereo photo series for quantifying natural fuels. Volume VIa: sand hill, sand pine scrub, and hardwood with white pine types in the Southeast United States with supplemental sites for Volume VI. PMS 838. Boise, ID: National Wildfire Coordinating Group, National Interagency Fire Center. 78 p.

Ottmar, R. D.; Vihnanek, R. E.; Regelbrugge, J. C. 2000. Stereo photo series for quantifying natural fuels. Volume IV: pinyon-juniper, sagebrush, and chaparral types in the Southwestern United States. PMS 833. Boise, ID: National Wildfire Coordinating Group, National Interagency Fire Center. 97 p.

Ottmar, R. D.; Vihnanek, R. E.; Wright, C. S. 1998. Stereo photo series for quantifying natural fuels. Volume I: mixed-conifer with mortality, western juniper, sagebrush, and grassland types in the Interior Pacific Northwest. PMS 830. Boise, ID: National Wildfire Coordinating Group, National Interagency Fire Center. 73 p.

Ottmar, R. D.; Vihnanek, R. E.; Wright, C. S. 2000. Stereo photo series for quantifying natural fuels. Volume III: lodgepole pine, quaking aspen, and gambel oak types in the Rocky Mountains. PMS 832. Boise, ID: National Wildfire Coordinating Group, National Interagency Fire Center. 85 p.

Ottmar, R. D.; Vihnanek, R. E.; Wright, C. S. 2002. Stereo photo series for quantifying natural fuels. Volume Va: jack pine in the Lake States. PMS 837. Boise, ID: National Wildfire Coordinating Group, National Interagency Fire Center. 49 p.

Rothermel, R. C. 1972. A mathematical model for predicting fire spread in wildland fuels. Res. Pap. INT-115. Ogden, UT: U.S. Department of Agriculture, Forest Service, Intermountain Forest and Range Experiment Station. 40 p.

Rothermel, R. C. 1983. How to predict the spread and intensity of forest and range fires. Gen. Tech. Rep. INT-143. Ogden, UT: U.S. Department of Agriculture, Forest Service, Intermountain Forest and Range Experiment Station. 161 p.

Van Wagner, C. E. 1977. Conditions for the start and spread of crown fire. Canadian Journal of Forest Research 7: 23-34.

Wright, C. S.; Ottmar, R. D.; Vihnanek, R. E.; Weise, D. R. 2002. Stereo photo series for quantifying natural fuels. Grassland, shrubland, woodland, and forest types in Hawaii. Gen. Tech Rep. PNW-GTR-545. Portland, OR: U.S. Department of Agriculture, Forest Service, Pacific Northwest Research Station. 91 p.